Soul Journeys with the Dying

Death is not something that simply happens to us at the end of life and which we have to undergo merely passively. Dying belongs to the very fabric of life. Each moment of life in which we find we are not in control and are forced to let go patiently nurtures seeds of a more profound experience of what it is to be human. Once we realise this, then death loses some of its sense of terror for us. Perhaps eventually we come to recognise that what we call death is really only the death of death itself. Accompanying people as they let go into the mystery of death is a great privilege, as the author of this book can testify. Paddy Pender shares her experiences of journeying with people in their final moments clearly and courageously. The book reassures us as we face our own inevitable experiences of loss. It also invites us to look for the risen among the dead, to look for the signs of new life even if all we can smell is decay.

Eamonn Conway, priest and theologian, Mary Immaculate College

The power of Paddy Pender's stories is that they are true. There is nothing more powerful that the truth, simple and unadorned. Anyone who reads them with the respect and attention that they deserve will be changed by them.

Alan McGuckian, SJ

Often it is only in its final stages that the purpose of life becomes clear. Through the stories shared over the course of these pages we are given rare glimpses into the meaning of life. In the tradition of *Tuesdays with Morrie*, this work shares Paddy Pender's own journey and brushes with mortality as she shares the final stages in the lives of people whose journey is nearing the end. Through her forthright honesty and attention to detail we are brought on a journey with the author to places we didn't know existed. On this journey we come to see a carer whose ministry to the ill and dying is characterised by humility, gentleness and care.

In a series of vignettes the author explores how illness and mortality are powerful catalysts in leading us to discovering the purpose of our lives. Through these pages we share the author's own journey through painful transitions and illness as she reaches out in support to others who are facing death.

Henry David Thoreau once wrote that the reason he went to live in the woods near Walden was that he "wished to live deliberately, to front only the essential facts of life, and see if I could not learn what it had to teach, and not, when I came to die, discover that I had not lived". Through her own encounter with illness and through her friendship with those who are dying, Paddy Pender encourages the reader to discover what illness and mortality have to teach us about the way we live our lives today.

Pat Farragher, director, The Family Centre, Castlebar

Best wishes
Paddy

Soul Journeys with the Dying

Soul Journeys with the Dying

PADDY PENDER

RED HEN PUBLISHING

Soul Journeys with the Dying
First published in 2007
by Red Hen Publishing,
Duagh, Listowel, Co Kerry, Ireland
www.redhen-publishing.com
Email: redhen1@eircom.net

Cover photography by Dieter Stark
Edited by Bridget McAuliffe, redhen1@eircom.net

A catalogue record of this book is available from the British Library
ISBN (10) 0-9552920-2-6
ISBN (13) 978-0-9552920-2-6

Printed in England
by J H Haynes & Co Ltd,
Sparkford, Somerset

Dedicated to my family
and especially to my father
who died at Christmas, 1992.

ACKNOWLEDGEMENTS

My sincere thanks to Una MacConville
for her constant encouragement
during the writing of this book;
to Pat and Valerie for their proof-reading skills
and helpful comments from the start of the project;
to Adrian, Clare, Jo, Ronan, DJ, Alan, Sr Stan, Robert, Joan
and the members of Anamcharadas for their assistance;
to Mary for the first journal;
to all those I have journeyed with
– particularly those I have mentioned in the stories.

CONTENTS

INTRODUCTION

They have eyes but they do not see[1]

Welcome. Before we start on our journey together, let me introduce myself. A child of the 1960s, I live and work in Dublin, the city I was born and reared in. I was given the name 'Paddy', a name normally reserved for males. In my case however, my arrival was announced to one of my uncles who then lived in London with, "John, you have a new niece, and she is a red head". In response he declared – "Well, another Irish Paddy is born". His words left a lasting impression on my parents and left me with a handle that I wouldn't change for the world. As a child I could see no problem with being called Paddy, but once I started school, there was considerable pressure on me to use a more formal name, which I declined to do.

From an early age, I loved puzzles and numerical problems. I rarely read books, but I always enjoyed stories and storytelling. I think I was about ten years of age when I decided I would like to be a mathematics teacher, and this desire became my focus until I left school seven years later. At twenty-one, I had a degree in mathematics and mathematical physics. A diploma in education would be the final step towards completing my dream, but at the information evening for those of us applying for teacher training,

1 Psalm 135:16

we were advised not to apply unless we were fully committed to the teenagers in our classes. I left the talk totally gutted because I knew I could never give that kind of commitment. With the support of my family, I stayed on in college and completed a masters degree in management science. I then went on to teach mathematics in university at tutorial level across a number of faculties. I loved college teaching but I knew it was only a temporary position for a couple of years. I knew I would have to find something more permanent, but during the 1980s in Ireland there were not many jobs for young graduates.

My mathematical side was balanced to some degree by a love of knitting, sewing and model-making. When my brothers got model-making kits, we often enjoyed building them together and I sometimes built the models for them. One summer I got a present of a BMW police motorbike kit. I spent weeks meticulously putting it together. All the moving parts worked, even the brakes. Because this was such a fragile piece of work, I decided to put it safely away on the top of the wardrobe where it could be admired at a safe distance. It lasted just a few days before someone slammed the bedroom door and it came crashing down. Needless to say, the brakes no longer work and it requires a considerable imagination to recognise the masterpiece it once was. Since the BMW incident, I have concentrated on sewing and knitting. They are much safer hobbies and the articles created generally last a lot longer than my poor bike.

My main focus was always mathematics, but I also studied computer programming for my post-graduate degree. Computer studies had only been introduced to third level education at that time, and the subject was very new to both staff and students. We were the 'computer kids' who cut our teeth on the old punch card systems and progressed from there. The growth in computer technology is so fast these days, I think it must be difficult for people to keep up, but back then, when I started, the pace was much slower. I found I had time to gain a good understanding of the software and the hardware before a new, improved model was introduced and this gave me a solid foundation to build on. With these mathematical and computer skills I sought employment in Ireland that would go some way towards fulfilling my dream. This all happened at a time when many of my friends were compelled to go overseas to find jobs and careers.

I felt very lucky and privileged when I got my ideal job with a real career path rather than part-time work and tutorials. I was totally energised by my work because it challenged me to fully use my computer skills and indeed to extend them continually. Before long, the job became a very significant part of my life and in time I was given responsibility for the training and support of computer users in the company. Many of my colleagues became good friends and over twenty years later, I am still in contact with some of them.

Every job has its trials and tribulations and mine was no different. The workplace was always extremely busy and often it was difficult to keep everything going. When I started working, there was one main computer with approximately thirty permanent users. A small user-base like this can be easily managed and it is relatively easy to keep the users up to date with new computer capabilities. Within a few short years, however, the number of computer users was well over three hundred, giving more than a few headaches to those of us who had to support them.

By the mid-nineties, most of the computer users were using personal computers linked to a main server. The introduction of the personal computer meant that individuals had full control of the computers on their desks. This is great for the computer literate, but for those who are not so literate it is a nightmare. As a computer trainer, my time was spent finding ways to give users easy access to computer facilities so that they could work efficiently. As computer capabilities grew and changed, so did the user capabilities and the user requirements. I found that I could no longer give any time to mathematics. The few grinds and tutorials I enjoyed giving had to give way almost entirely to the computer work.

I wasn't conscious of losing mathematics in my life because I was enjoying solving computer problems so much. I loved finding ways of teaching computer skills to others and I spent time putting together manuals and information sheets. As this organisational and computerised side of me developed, I spent more and more time working on a computer and less time with people. I spent an inordinate amount of time in front of a computer screen and this over-exposure took its toll. It's important to remember that health and safety issues were not considered that relevant when I started my computer career. What is taken as a norm nowadays was simply not heard of back then.

I suffered from frequent headaches and my eyes tired easily and became very painful. In time I found I wasn't able to see as clearly as I ought to. I had my glasses checked and some adjustments were made to my prescription lenses. While this seemed to work at first, it was not long before the problems reoccurred. I wore special shades on my glasses to help reduce glare, but unfortunately the positive effects were shortlived. Finally, I was advised that I would have to reduce the number of hours in front of the computer screen. I tried doing this over a period of months, but the work built up significantly, increasing the pressure on me and resulting in more headaches and raised stress levels. I was caught in a vicious cycle that I could not break, but one that was breaking me.

At this time I lost control of my eye muscles and the two eyes worked at different rates. This meant I saw two images in two dimensions, with one image on top of the other but slightly to the right. It may sound confusing, but try viewing a slide through a slide projector and then get a copy of the slide and view it through a second projector that is a fraction to the right and above the first. The only way to see the image properly is to remove one of the slide projectors. For me to properly see what I was looking at, I had to close one of my eyes.

Walking around with one eye closed looks ridiculous, so I developed a way of cutting off the sight in one eye so that I could keep the two eyes open and still see only one image. I alternated the 'seeing eye' so that both eyes were working at the same strength and neither one got lazy. A time came when this system failed me and I could no longer control the eyes. I had to physically cover one of my eyes, but this put horrendous pressure on the other eye.

The headaches were intolerable and eventually I was told that the only way to improve my sight was to take a complete break from computer work and put a lot of effort into distance work rather than close work. For six months, I had to rest, take walks to help improve my distance vision with no computers, minimal television, no knitting, sewing or reading. I was not allowed to cover one eye at any time and I was not to consciously shut off the vision in either eye at all. This meant I often saw two floating images so I had an almost permanent feeling similar to sea-sickness. I realised that while I was doing my best to have my eyesight repaired, rumours about my visual problems abounded and in time I discovered that many thought I was going blind. Personally, I believed in my heart that the six months of rest would do the trick and I would be back at work by the beginning of the seventh month. Believing this helped me get through this difficult time and through the weeks leading up to my departure from work. During my sick leave I had so much extra time on my hands I found it difficult to fill the day.

I could not enjoy any of my hobbies and I sought out jobs I could undertake in order to get exercise. I would walk three miles to drop off a letter and then walk another three miles home. Such a task would fulfil the exercise requirement while also helping me feel I still had a purpose in life. My job had been my life, but this had been taken away suddenly and cruelly. I was willing now to take on any task, no matter how small, or how seemingly menial.

One of the tasks I undertook in the early days was picking up post for a family friend, Tom, and bringing it to him. As his health deteriorated, I became one of his regular visitors and when he moved to a nursing home, I continued visiting him up until his death. I found that a new life started for me as Tom's life started to leave him. I remember a close friend commenting that I had changed and, without thinking, I told him I had died and a new person was born into the same body.

Once I recognised and accepted this death, and the new life it presented me with, I started really living. The greatest surprise was the fact that I liked this new life a lot more than the precious computer career that I had put on a high pedestal. As I recalled the comment of a former colleague – "you'll never be anything but a computer career woman" – I wondered how I had allowed myself to be so boxed into a career for so long. At all times during my sick leave, however, my goal was simply to get well and return to work.

I was willing to do whatever was prescribed even though I was anxious that it might require surgery or a hospital stay. I have a great fear of hospitals, which was not helped by the fact that I was told I would be scheduled for surgery if there wasn't a significant improvement in my eye function within three months. I worked hard to meet this target but my eyesight did not improve. I had successful surgery on both eyes four months after I left work and was back using computers on a limited basis within a month of the surgery. However, my attempts to build up my computer hours so that I could return to work were fruitless. My sick pay was halved at the end of the first six months and was terminated at the end of one year. For two years I had to rely on family and some state support. Financially, times were very difficult.

Within three years of my departure I resigned from my full-time computer career. The decision to resign was one of the most difficult things I had to do. I cannot describe the sense of loss and the feelings of abandonment and disappointment that I felt when I came to this decision. I thought I would not be able to cope. But I confess that the day I signed the resignation form was one of the most freeing days of my life. For the first time, I let go of the attachment to my career and to my perceived status among family and friends. The reaction of those around me was one of surprise and worry. My new interests did not provide a regular income, but I was willing to take a risk. It had become clear that returning to my career was unattainable and I decided that it was time to fully let go.

New opportunities opened up for me from a number of quarters. I continued helping out in the nursing home where my friend Tom had been, I started part-time parish work and I also developed a small business. At the outset of this significant time of change in my life, in fact on the day I started my sick leave, I was given a present of a journal. With some trepidation, I committed my most sacred thoughts and emotions to this book and then to another journal, and to another journal.

On occasion, I would venture to cast an eye over my writings and all I had survived. I found in these pages the courageous voice of a survivor, rather than a report of events and mishaps. I found consolation, hope and encouragement in what I read. I found lesson after lesson, many of which I only became aware of as I read over the pages and brought the events and relationships back to life. I never felt the writing as a burden or a chore, but rather as a wonderful way of letting off steam when times were rough, and also as a sacred place for recording precious moments when times were good.

During all this time my faith sustained me. Despite using my journals to honestly let God know just how angry I was that so many challenges had been presented to me in what appeared to be such a short time, I still could not turn away from the beliefs I held since childhood. I believe these times helped develop and even strengthen my faith. The icing on the cake for me came was when I was offered a place on a programme to train as an Anam Chara. This came within a month of signing my resignation and the training helped me see just how important my spiritual life was.

There was a time when I packaged my faith life into the weekly church services and tried to live the rest of my life as if I was on a solo run. Time and the events that were presented to me taught me the importance of allowing my spiritual life blend more smoothly with my ordinary daily life. I now see how my need for non-visual activities during the early months led to many opportunities I had never considered before. The chain of events, from getting involved with visiting the sick and parish work, to working with the homeless and then completing my training as an Anamchara, was not a coincidence, but rather a divine plan for me. Today, I am happily involved in each of these areas and I also continue to train computer users on a one-to-one basis.

In conversation I shared some of my stories with others and, with their encouragement, I have written about my personal journey using my journals, Scripture and personal stories. As we set out together on this journey, I can physically see very little of what is around me but I am learning to see through what I hear and what I perceive. I relate the stories in the present tense so that we can walk together in the Now.

MY INVITATION TO YOU

Did not my heart burn inside[1]

You are invited to walk with me on my personal journey and meet some of the people who, in their own way, open my eyes to the endless possibilities that life and death present. They teach me that there is great life in another's dying. They teach me to see nature with new eyes. They open my senses, my heart, my soul, and show me the truth in John's Gospel where he writes:

Very truly, I tell you, unless a grain of wheat falls into the earth and dies, it remains just a single grain; but if it dies, it bears much fruit.[2]

I survive the death of my father by burying myself in a state of busyness and do not see any of the possibilities that his death opens up. I am unaware of the effects of losing myself in this busyness until four years later, when I find myself starting out on a very new part of my journey in life. Often I wonder when it all started. I wonder about a day and a date. Whenever I ponder on this I immediately think of two particular days. The first is a Friday in early September and I am at a friend's wedding. Unusually, the

---

1 Luke 24:32
2 John 12:24

weather is very good and the sun is high and strong. It is a great day for a wedding and I am having a wonderful time. My wedding present to the couple is a video of the day, so I arrive early to set up my cameras and catch everyone on film as they arrive. The camera gives me permission to mingle fully with family, friends and strangers alike. Of course, there are those who would rather I put the camera away, but while I'm on duty I catch as many moments as possible. The surprisingly good weather for the time of year gives me extra energy, but by the end of the celebrations I suddenly feel de-energised.

Travelling back home I find the driving difficult. I feel tired. My eyes hurt and I have to concentrate very hard to keep them in focus. I often feel like this at the end of a hard day at work and expect my sight to improve with a good night's sleep. The sleep helps, but there is still some discomfort. I return to work on the Monday morning as expected, but within a week I notice a significant deterioration in my vision. I consult my eye specialist who advises taking time off to allow my eyes heal and suggests I may need surgery. Reluctantly, I follow this advice.

The second significant day is a Friday at the end of the same September. It is my last day in work, although at the time I thought it was simply the first day of my sick leave. I arrive in the office to hear the sad news of the sudden death of a senior member of staff. There is a moving memorial service after which I am suddenly aware that death does not always mean the end of a life, but that it can simply mean a change in one's being.

As I leave the memorial service, a colleague quietly wishes me well and tells me he hopes that I am soon back to full health. I break down sobbing and as he puts his arm around me to comfort me, I begin to see my eye problems as a major death in my own life. For the first time since childhood, I feel vulnerable and alone.

I don't like the feeling and grow ever more anxious as I return to the office. Wiping away the tears I allow people assume that I am upset at the death of my colleague. Only I know the truth about these tears and the fears and anxieties that they hide.

My departure is low key and does not prepare me for the utter sense of loss at not being able to go to work. Days are very long when the routine is broken, especially when the new routine is a lot slower and less intellectually challenging. On this same Friday, I arrive home to hear that a young friend of the family is killed in a road traffic accident. Soon after this sad news, I get a phone call from a close friend to let me know that a mutual friend of ours has died by suicide. Even soap-operas cannot cram so much disaster into an episode, but this truly was that Friday in September. My visual problems pale into insignificance when all this is happening, but my gut tells me that these tragedies are markers for rough times ahead for me. My gut is not wrong on this weekend, but facing into each of the memorial services helps me understand the fragility of life and the inevitability of death. I also accept that tragedies such as these can happen to anyone and I brace myself for the possibility that everything does not have to happen to my plan, but that unforeseen circumstances can and will appear.

It becomes apparent to me that I have been using my work as a way of hiding from my grief, pain and losses. For the first time since my father's death, I am launched out into the deep, into a new world. Just as my eyes are failing me, I become aware of a deeper blindness which must have been part of my life for a long time. I grope in the dark inside and outside. The journey you are about to join me on starts as I strive to find my rightful place in this new world. During this transition, I have old and new friends with me. Old friends such as Brian and Tom offer me comfort immediately after my bereavement following my father's death and, in time, I find myself offering comfort to them as their lives draw to a close.

Looking back now, I see the obvious patchwork of learning and teaching of which we were all a part. I am taking one day at a time, moving on in blind faith. I am often the unwilling student, hoping I can take a break from all the lessons. But the lessons go on every single day and today I am very happy and grateful for the education I receive. My teachers are all those I meet during the ordinary comings and goings of my daily activities. The most important lessons are often learned at the feet of those who are close to their own death. The classroom is our shared lives at these crucial times.

There are hidden links between the people you are going to meet. Some of the links are obvious now, but at the time they were completely invisible to me. Trust in others plummeted when my father died and drops even more when my eyesight fails.

Shortly after my new routine starts and while my trust levels are at an all-time low, I am asked to visit Tom and check that he is well. Tom is an old family friend who has been ill of late. Soon I become a regular visitor and he grows to trust me and gives me permission to share his last weeks with him despite the fact that our relationship prior to his illness is based on respect, tinged with fun.

Mark is totally unknown to me, yet he and I share at a very deep level. He arrives into my life at a time when I am beginning to realise that I may not be able to return to my computer career. The overlap in our lives is also a precursor for a journey I later make with an old friend, Brian. The experiences with Tom, Mark and Brian prepare me for my subsequent training in Anamcharadas to become an Anam Chara (soul friend). Natalie and I share just a short time together and although we exchange very few words, she teaches me some hard facts about life in our world today.

Finally, Peggy is in my life through all the stages of this journey. She is often in the background, coming to the fore every now and then, allowing our two lives to merge and separate as in the weave of a cloth.

Through the stages of my journey I look to my faith for support and am upset when the good news I hope for does not materialise. Even when I eventually lose my lovely job after almost three years of waiting, hoping and struggling my way back to health, I look beyond the disappointment to see the bigger picture. During this time I have a strong sense that God is working with me, but I never anticipate the huge changes ahead and certainly would not have voluntarily chosen the track God has me on.

Within months of losing my job, I am invited to apply for a place on a training programme with Anamcharadas. The timing is just right for me so I apply and am successful. The training and sharing with the other participants on the programme afford me a space to really reflect on my inner journey and the impact various events have on it. The tradition of having an Anam Chara goes back to the foundation of the monasteries in Ireland. Hundreds of years ago, people often sought advice, consolation and guidance from an Anam Chara and as the practice grew it became a feature of monastic and Christian life.

Today, people continue to seek out an Anam Chara to companion them on their inner journey in life. The importance of having space to talk and feel heard is as relevant today as it was in monastic times. This listening ministry takes place in many different places. My own ministry sometimes takes place on a busy street or in a bustling shopping centre but very often it takes place in a quiet room. I look to the Scriptures for answers and I journal the answers I find there. It is a difficult but wonderful time once I open myself up to the new challenges set before me and the new people sent to help me through them. I recognise a very subtle change in myself when I see my heart rather than my head dictating my life. This is my unfolding, the peeling back of the layers to get to my heart.

There are common threads in what you will read. The first is that "I cannot do this without help from a source that is much greater than me".[3] This source is my creator who makes all of humankind and the universe I enjoy and destroy. The second thread is that "I am a link in a chain, a bond of connection between persons".[4] Just as I see myself as a link in a chain, the people you will meet are other links in this chain. The following reflection of Cardinal Newman helps me to see more clearly that I am not alone. It is a great source of comfort and support for me as I unfold.

God has created me to do Him some definite service; He committed some work to me which He has not committed to another. I have my mission – I may never know it in this life, but I shall be told it in the next. I am a link in a chain, a bond of connection between persons. He has not created me for naught. I shall do good; I shall do His work. I shall be an angel of peace, a preacher of truth in my own place while not intending it – if I do but keep His commandments. Therefore I will trust Him. Whatever, wherever I am, I can never be thrown away. If I am in sickness, my sickness may serve Him; in perplexity, my perplexity may serve Him. He does nothing in vain. He knows what He is about. He may take away my friends. He may throw me among strangers. He may make me feel desolate, make my spirits sink, hide my future from me – still he knows what He is about.[5]

---

3 Personal Journal, 8 February 1997

4 Newman, Cardinal John Henry. *Meditations on Christian Doctrine; Hope in God*, 6 March 1848

5 Newman, Cardinal John Henry. *Meditations on Christian Doctrine; Hope in God*, 6 March 1848

Throughout the stories, I am conscious that the things I do and the events I am part of are not of my doing alone. They come about only when I let go and trust in God. It isn't easy for me and I am often afraid, but I always come through in one piece and am spiritually a much stronger person. I experience great sadness matched with unbelievable joy. My heart sometimes feels close to bursting from the pain and heartbreak, only to be replenished with peace and calm. Everything of myself that I think I am giving to another comes back to me a hundred-fold and gift-wrapped.

I heard a story once about a saint who is said to have chastised God following the loss of most of the supplies she was transporting to a new monastery. The response she heard from God when she asked "Why?" was that He did it because "You are my friend". "Well," she responds, "if that's the way you treat your friends, I'm not surprised you don't have many." I could have written these words myself on many occasions. I often have serious words with God when I feel too challenged by yet another dilemma I believe He has set before me. However, we are still on speaking terms, leaving room for more dilemmas, more arguing and more making up.

I used to ask questions like "why?" but now I see how this type of question restricts my options so I am more inclined to ask "How am I to see this one through?" I learn on this journey that I am never alone and that I can see any challenge through to its end when I trust. I am able to see the importance of events that once I would have considered mere coincidences.

I am reminded of the story of the man arriving in heaven, disappointed that God let him down by not coming down to earth to save him. God responds, reminding him that He sent a variety of people to help, but the man turned down their offers of help. I never expect God to appear at my side dressed in the fashion of two thousand years ago, looking like the images which adorn the walls of the art galleries and churches throughout the world. I expect God to come dressed in regular clothes and in the shape of a neighbour, friend and stranger alike, and I am never disappointed. Just like my friend in the story, however, I don't always recognise God's helping hand. The movies provide violin music to prompt viewers that something ethereal is happening, but real life is different. I have to be open to all the possibilities around me and to trust.

No matter how difficult things are, no matter how often I want to walk away and shout "I've had enough – get someone else to take over", I get a rush of energy that brings me over my doubts into a new space. It feels like a dance of butterflies in my stomach and their battle-cry is non-verbal encouragement to take the necessary steps to go on. Sometimes when I open a book or hear a piece of Scripture, I find the answer to my plea for relief and I receive the support I need to take the next step. It is in the unexpected that I see others coming to rescue me. The rescue vessels come through well-known friends and complete strangers alike. I don't know why I bother arguing with God, because He always gets his own way in the end. I feel like I'm just wasting my energy arguing, but I do enjoy the banter. I heard this poem of St Teresa read out one day and in a matter of weeks I heard it being sung. At that time, I was experiencing quite a few challenges, but as I listened I heard the answers to the 'why, when and where?' questions I had put before God at the time.

Christ has no body now but yours
No hands, no feet on earth but yours
Yours are the eyes through which he looks
Compassion on this world
Yours are the feet with which he walks to do good

Yours are the hands with which he blesses all the world
Yours are the hands, yours are the feet, yours are the eyes,
You are his body.[6]

As I reflect on the words, they are sometimes beyond my reach. They seem like an impossible list of instructions, but every now and then, I look at just one line at a time and before long I can accept the whole poem. The greatest gift coming from it for me is the knowledge that Christ is continually working in and through all of humankind, even me. Now the poem is a source of great comfort and encouragement, and it also invites me to see all of humankind in a new and different way. The poem also reminds me that Christ died and is risen, and lives in and through everyone I meet. Each of the journeys in the following sections is a testament to this resurrected Christ; the same resurrected Christ that Mary Magdalene met outside the tomb.

During our lives on earth we die many times and rise again before dying fully to this earthly life. During her journey on earth Mary Magdalene changed her way of life following her meeting with Jesus. She died to her former life and became a new person and a very close friend of Jesus. I have no doubt that Mary Magdalene suffered the scorn and unworthy comments of others who could see her only in her former role. Many would not have been open to seeing her transformation. I believe she must have suffered greatly and must have sacrificed much to maintain her new way of life. This is a very real death fully accompanied by its grief, but it is also a wonderful new birth.

When Jesus died, Mary Magdalene experienced the pain and heartbreak of losing her friend, just as any one of us would. I often imagine the fear and anxiety she must have felt as she

---

6 Teresa of Avila (1515–1582) Christ Has No Body

approached the empty tomb. Blinded by her pain, she eventually recognised Jesus when he called her by her name[7]. Our names are so important to us and being called by name is a special way of indicating that our attention is required and that another wants to engage with us and be available to us.

The prophet Isaiah tells us not to be afraid because we have been called by name by God and he assures us of God's love for each and every one of us . Following Mary Magdalene's meeting with Jesus, we hear how the hearts of the two disciples on the road to Emmaus burned within them as they listened to Jesus, but only recognised him moments before he disappeared from their sight. I often fail to recognise my friends until I stop and hear my name being called out. I walk each day on journeys similar to the Emmaus journey and, most of the time, I am not aware of Jesus walking with me. Life is busy and there are so many things to be doing, I am blinded to Jesus in the middle of all my comings and goings. But blind or not, Jesus is in the middle of it – good, bad and indifferent.

These passages from the Old Testament and New Testament are as alive today as they were when they were first written. I know this to be true because I, too, weep at the tombs of friends; I, too, walk many roads and listen and feel my heart on fire; I, too, know the pain of deaths in my life and the subsequent new births. I know these things through the people I walk with and the wonderful insights they give me about myself.

The stories you are about to read are events that I am privileged to be part of and are very like the encounters from Scripture. Scripture is not just a history of what happened two thousand years ago. It is real life, here and now. It is my life, here and now. I have yet to find a passage in Scripture that does not reflect some part of my life and my very being. I see myself in the stories and

7 John 20:14-16

in the people, whether or not I like what I see. I know that the answers to my questions are there for me to find – all I have to do is look. I don't always like what I find, but it is there nonetheless.

As I look at the Scriptures, I see the great number of times people like Simon Peter and Mary Magdalene took risks to follow their hearts. I often envy their courage and commitment, only to find similar courage and commitment all around me. Indeed there are times when I find myself plucking up the courage to do something different and I can now acknowledge that I, too, take risks. Just as the apostles took the risk and left their nets to follow into the unknown, I take risks and go out into my unknown. There is great comfort knowing that anything I have to face has already been written about in Scripture. It is all about relationships, about love. My stories are love stories – God's love in all of us, God's love in all of his creation, which includes every single person and the entire universe.

As my story unfolds, my reluctance to accept this unfolding is apparent, but the gratitude I feel at having accepted it is beyond words.

TOM

Unless a grain of wheat should fall to the earth[1]

Autumn is my favourite season since it is neither too cold nor too warm. The days are still long and bright enough to enjoy a good walk. There is a sense of cosiness as fires are lit in many homes. I always think of it as a very welcoming season. However, this particular autumn, I am not so happy. I am finding it hard to endure the days while I am unable to go to work. I fill my days with short walks and very limited visual work. This means I need to ration my television viewing and can do no computer work. I quickly volunteer to do errands for family and friends just to keep myself occupied.

One evening, my mother tells me that our friend Tom is not well at all and that she is very worried about him. I can understand her concern and helplessness, but wonder at what she or I can do. Earlier in the day he was talking on the phone to one of his relatives when the phone went dead. The caller thought he had died and asked that he be checked on. Without a key to gain access I am not sure what to do. I have visions of the emergency services coming and breaking into his apartment, so I decide to visit myself and then phone for the emergency services if they are needed. One voice in me questions the visit on the grounds

---

1 John 12:24

that it is alarmist and intrusive. Another voice urges me to face my fears at the possibility of finding him lying sick, dying or dead in his home. Feeling quite helpless, I arrange to meet up with one of the local priests, Fr John. Tom knows him quite well and I feel more comfortable having someone with me. The closer we get to Tom's home, the more I am convinced of the worst.

We gingerly knock on the door and, lo and behold, a small stooped figure is visible through the frosted glass. Tom opens it. He looks as if he has just woken him from a nap and appears anxious and confused by our visit. He leads us into his sitting room and takes a seat near the fire. Despite the fire, the room is barely warm. Fr John sits close to Tom and I take a seat on the opposite side of the room. He looks tired and unwell, but better than I expect. I leave the two men to their conversation and I observe Tom's surroundings.

The room is large and filled with beautiful old furniture. I imagine the dresser is full of the history of Tom's life. There is silverware acknowledging his work with a variety of organisations. There is a television, video and music system. The videos are neatly stacked and indexed, as are all his music tapes. Tom is an avid fan of musicals and light opera, and enjoys these when there is no soccer to be watched. Photographs adorn the walls, giving a few more glimpses of his interests and pastimes. I learn a lot about Tom just looking around the room and listening to himself and Fr John chatting.

Every now and then, Tom looks directly at me and acknowledges my presence without uttering a word. He is curious as to why we have called, but doesn't say too much. He appears to be too tired to ask questions and is inclined to fall asleep while he is talking. As we laugh and joke about football and the state of the nation, I begin to relax in my chair and enjoy watching Tom as he puts so much energy into our visit. Up to this, he and I have normally shared a rather jocose form of communication, but as I observe, I am aware of a new, deeper connection between us. He watches me closely and smiles approvingly every now and then. It is as though the fun layer has been peeled away and we have moved into a new kind of relationship.

Watching Tom, I am a very relieved that he is alive, but I am also aware that all is not well. He has been in poor health in recent months but never talks about his illness. He is a very private man, in his late sixties, but tonight, sitting in his armchair, he looks so small and frail. The fire brings no glow to Tom's pale cheeks. He becomes listless and distant despite being aware of our presence. Although he is normally a hospitable person, he neglects to offer us a beverage of any sort.

My relationship with Tom is one of 'friend of the family'. He is someone who visits the family home often and shares an entertaining evening in the company of my parents and their friends. He has, in fact, always been part of our family and yet I know only facts about him. I know where he lives and where he works. I know that he loves soccer and is a senior member of the management of one of the local teams. I know he is now semi-retired from his own business. I know that he is a God-fearing, church-going believer. About the person that he really is, I know nothing.

As I sit listening to Tom chatting, I feel less of an alarmist or intruder. Making the visit is an important step for me and for Fr John. In the first place, it demonstrates to Tom that we care about him and that we are offering a helping hand. No one in the room has any idea of what is ahead, but my gut feeling on this first evening is that we are setting out on a road together. Leaving Tom's home, Fr John and I are concerned about practical things such as the fact that Tom is not looking after himself properly and that he is sleeping so much. I am concerned about how we will deal with these facts. The fear of what we might find that evening is now replaced by a determination to stay close to Tom through his illness which I suspect is very serious. I wonder how long he can survive without taking more care of himself. I want to say that it is not my problem, but I can't. I feel part of his life and world now, invited or not. I have a strong feeling that it is meant to be. I have no idea how it feels for Tom, but for me:

My heart is racing at all that has happened in just a few short hours. I don't know how I feel about calling to Tom. I wonder tonight about the bigger picture and how the two of us fit into it. I don't believe this incident is the end of the story – it feels like the beginning of something big. I hope I will be able for the next step.[2]

Within days, Tom surprises us all by getting into his car and driving to England and Wales to visit his relatives. Despite being very ill and despite our protestations, he insists on making the trip. Alone, Tom drives ten miles to the ferry terminal, boards the ferry and, hours later, disembarks on the other side with the help of the port staff. How he manages to drive through the night to his relatives we will never know. We believe his guardian angels are working overtime during these days. I have often heard of seriously ill people making incredible efforts to visit friends and relatives in order to say goodbye in person. It can defy medical science, but can certainly give closure to those involved. It is a real gift when it is possible.

Something deep down in Tom tells him he will not make Christmas so he brings Christmas forward a few months. I don't believe Tom could get his head around the fact he is ill, but I believe his heart knows. And it is wonderful for him to experience the

2 Personal Journal, 14 October 1996

kindness of complete strangers who come to his assistance, getting his car on and off the boats, and the Lord knows what else.

Tom looks so unwell and yet he ventures off on the boat by himself. Is Tom dying and is he realising it at a heart level? He certainly doesn't talk about it if he is. If he is dying, am I going to be able to stay the course with him? Is that where that first night is leading us? I don't like all this guessing. I imagine Jesus felt something like this when he knew he would die soon but also knew he couldn't turn back. This is not nice and I would prefer someone else to be here instead of me. Am I Simon of Cyrene refusing to take the cross or Veronica moving forward with the towel? I want to be like Veronica, but – can I do it? I can't if I rely solely on my own resources. It was a power greater than myself that allowed me call to Tom that first night and I have to believe that God isn't going to leave me now.[3]

As much as I am relieved that Tom did not die alone in his home that first night, I am more relieved to hear he is back home safe and sound, following a successful visit across the Irish Sea. He is not well, however. Two very close friends, Jim and Simon, meet Tom when he gets back and encourage him to get medical help. As soon as he agrees, they take him to hospital. After some negotiation with the hospital authorities, Tom is eventually admitted.

In less that one month, he has deteriorated so much he is barely able to do anything for himself. He is angry at being admitted to hospital, angry at being ill, angry with Jim and Simon, angry with all of us who try to help in any way. Jim and Simon, however, are not willing to allow him home to live alone and probably die alone. It is one of those dreadful situations where the practicalities take over, and the desires of the individual are put aside. It is a very hard one to call, because it brings up guilt and betrayal

3 Personal Journal, 31 October 1996

for ourselves as friends while we know there is no other option – the choice-less choice. I am not very good at accepting help when I am unwell and can empathise with Tom in his current situation. When I am sick, I know I have to put myself in the hands of doctors, carers and family to ensure my well-being, even though I really don't want to. I am independent to the point of sheer stubbornness, cherishing my own space and privacy. These personality traits are clearly evident in Tom and I imagine he is filled with a similar level of fear and anxiety as I would be if I were admitted to hospital against my will. At another level, he may be pleased that his friends care so much about him that they go out of their way to see he is cared for. Personally, I feel helpless and sometimes hopeless in all of this.

From the time Tom is admitted to hospital, my walking route includes regular calls to his office on the way to visit him, to pick up the post and the news of the place. At the office there is always a brief exchange about how Tom is and the changes we have noticed on our visits. We are all looking for something positive to do for him, but it isn't easy for any of us. I keep in touch with Fr John, my companion from that first evening. It feels like I am on a roller-coaster of emotions, wanting to be at home, away from all the sickness and misery, yet drawn to sit with Tom for some time each day on the off-chance that I may be of use.

As I approach the hospital, I grow anxious about how he is going to be with me. Walking through the automatic doors, there is the familiar smell of disinfectant and furniture polish. It's strange, but the smell strikes me so much each time. It is absolute confirmation that I am entering the world of Tom's illness. When I reach the four-bed ward, I look for Tom and find him half asleep on his bed. He looks smaller than ever when he is in bed and, as I sit and wait with him, I wonder about the way I sit and do nothing, but of course, sitting is doing something. I discover that just being with him is much more important than trying to do things for him. Tom often glances over and simply smiles at me. I love the smile and all I can do is smile back as I lean forward to see if he is going to say something. He has little or no energy for doing anything. What is there to do when time is short and so precious? I never want him to think that no one cares.

He smiles as he recognises me – I love that. He is very weak and hardly able to talk. A visitor lightly tipped him on the hand and he winced with the pain. All the way home, carrying his bag of washing, I could not get the image of this very tiny, feeble man out of my mind. The pain etched on his face breaks my heart and then there are times when he can look so peaceful.[4]

On one afternoon there is a strong smell in the ward as I walk in. It is very powerful and almost stifling. Tom does not seem to notice, but I can't bear it. At first I think he has soiled the bed but I'm relieved when he gets up to go to the bathroom and note that he hasn't. When he is in the bathroom, I check around the bed for the source of the smell. There is a vase of chrysanthemums on the locker and the water is stagnant, leaving the strong odour. The smell stays with me for the rest of the day and every time I come across chrysanthemums, it evokes a memory of that afternoon.

Tom rarely names the illness he has, but he knows deep down that it is the dreaded cancer. Most of his pain and discomfort is in the throat and it is confirmed by one of his relatives that he has oesophageal cancer. I call in one Sunday morning and when I get to the ward, there is no sign of Tom. He is sitting in the conservatory enjoying the sunshine while he waits for his lunch. The lunch of roast beef, vegetables and potatoes arrives and he

4 Personal Journal, 1 November 1996

allows me feed him. The roast beef is too difficult to eat so he reluctantly takes some of the mashed potato. As Tom takes the food, his stomach gurgles. He looks into my eyes and says, "I don't know when all this started, I don't have a date, but I call it 'the day of the body snatchers'". I have to look away as my eyes fill up. He takes some more food and his stomach gurgles again. Quietly, he says, "There they go again, fighting over every bit I put into my mouth". In his conversation, Tom is very visual about his illness and I find the images help me to get some sense of what might be happening for him. I say 'might', because it is impossible to know how he is really coping with all of this.

On my walks to and from the hospital I reflect a lot on the lack of future for Tom. Knowing that he will soon die makes the waiting all the more difficult. I want to know when the end will come, yet I don't want the end to arrive. It is a very confusing place. Part of me longs for some hope of recovery or even an easing of the symptoms. Neither will happen and suddenly the phrase 'you wouldn't leave an animal in such pain' comes to mind. What I am really thinking about is euthanasia but I won't name it – I call it the 'pillow job'.

I cannot believe how my mind turns over so many different thoughts. Things I believe in are being challenged and I am no longer absolutely confident in my faith. I have taken so much for granted, but this time with Tom is really pushing me. As I watch him drift away, I am fighting with God over the manner in which he is dying. I am angry about the pain. I am angry about feeling so lonely and alone. I am angry that I was chosen to be with Tom. I want peace and normality restored. I want my nice beliefs back in place – just as they were when I was a child in school, learning the Catechism. But those days are long gone, and I am living in a different time and place. I have to take the focus off me and back to Tom and his life. He is helping me to see more than I ever thought was out there. He is helping me to see more than I ever thought was in me. It is all revelation. I am afraid, but every time I am afraid a new person appears to put me back on track. God, I am so lucky that when I am challenged, an answer appears in the friends and strangers I meet – provided I open my eyes to see them and my ears to hear them.[5]

Walking home through the city streets trying not to think about the 'pillow job', I meet a friend who enquires after Tom. I respond quite sharply, saying "I'm getting awfully close to the 'pillow job'". The comment is met with a concerned look and a quick response of "But we don't believe in that. It is not an option for us". I really needed to hear that just at that time. He and I talk for a while and it becomes very clear to me that the 'pillow job' would only temporarily ease the pain I am suffering and would interfere with the course of Tom's life and death. It is, quite simply, not a choice that I have a right to make. Tom's religious upbringing teaches him to accept all suffering as a gift from God and as a symbol of his sharing in the death and resurrection of Jesus. I have a sense from what he says that he believes his illness and pain are punishments in atonement for past transgressions. If he does, his vision of God is very different from mine.

I rarely talk about God or religion with him. I don't feel comfortable talking about something as personal as faith. Trying so hard to understand all that is happening to this man leaves me feeling sad and helpless. I know that my God is not one to mete out punishments and certainly not the kind of punishment Tom is enduring. He accepts his 'punishment' freely and daily refuses painkillers from the medical staff. He believes he has to feel and suffer the pain. I become quite upset with him on occasions and

5 Personal Journal, 18 November 1996

plead with him to take the medication. I find it so difficult to accept his choice. The nurses, however, accept it and are able to walk away. I don't feel I can walk away. I tell him I cannot endure him writhing in pain when something can be done, but he quietly persists. Frustrated and upset by his insistence, I leave the hospital feeling tearful. It is only later that I see why he makes this decision and I accept it, albeit reluctantly. My pleading is about my own discomfort at watching him and does not acknowledge his desire to accept his pain.

I long for a time to be able to talk to Tom about a God who loves and cares and not about a God who punishes. All around us we see pain and suffering but this is human life – not the result of God dealing out sentences to the guilty who stand before him for judgement. I walk home from the hospital with a strong sense that I have met God in ALL the people I encounter during the day. More than that, I see God in the autumn moonlight and the wonderful starry nights. It's getting cold and people are planning Christmas. Me – I'm thinking about a friend who won't see this Christmas, but who will be part of my Christmas in a way I never imagined. The Litany of Remembrance is being drummed out these days as people remember war heroes. The line 'for they are now part of us and we remember them' keeps coming to me. Tom and I are on a journey – he is now part of me and I am part of him. This is the two of us on the road to Emmaus and as we grow more trusting of each other, it is like the third person joining us and opening up the meaning of life, living and dying to us. I am so lucky I took the risk in October so that I can be here today. I am also very afraid and very sad.[6]

Tom's demeanour is different and he is handling his illness in a new way. I'm not sure if it is acceptance on his part and a letting go. It is certainly like a 'change in life' that I imagine to be the beginning of

6 Personal Journal, 19 November 1996

his dying. It is his passage from this world to the next. I see myself being left behind on the quayside, waving goodbye as he sets sail on a voyage. As the image develops, I know in my heart that this is a voyage he won't be returning from. Other images come to mind during these days and in the middle of my confusion and anxiety, sadness and helplessness consume me.

I am upset and frustrated at not knowing what to say to Tom. He now talks to me about the cancer but lets on to others that it is 'old age'. To a certain extent, I feel so privileged to be there when he talks honestly and openly...I told a friend that Tom was very bad and that they [hospital staff] were looking for a bed for him in a nursing home. I can say the words so easily. My wish is that he will die peacefully with someone by his side who cares about him.[7]

The hospital we are in is a general hospital and we have been told that, medically, they can do no more for Tom. Since hospital beds are at a premium, a bed is being sought for Tom in a nursing home and he will move there when one becomes available. The hospital staff puts the bleak scenario to us in one brief session. There is little time to assimilate the information and actually come to terms with the reality of the prognosis.

The concept of moving from the hospital seems like a death sentence to me. It feels like Tom and I are moving onto Death Row and I am afraid that I will not be brave enough to stay with him until the end. I recall hearing about a woman who stayed with a Death Row inmate until he was executed. My lasting memory about the story was the eye-contact between the two as he lay strapped on the table, and I am comforted to hear of her tears – tears acknowledging her bravery and perseverance, and tears of sadness at the parting. The move for me is a bit like giving up on all the medication,

7 Personal Journal, 19 November 1996

technology and science, and giving up on Tom. But in reality, the move makes way for another patient to benefit from the expertise in the general hospital, while Tom moves aside to be looked after at a different level, with medication to help ease the symptoms.

Tom talks to very few people now. He has cut many out of his life and has made it clear who he will allow to visit and who he does not want. I am filled with tension and anxieties. I am overwhelmed on occasion by the trust he places in me. Each time I visit him, I brace myself as I enter the hospital. Walking in from the cold to the heat of the hospital makes my cheeks glow and most imagine me to be a healthy, together person, and not the anxious, nervous and stressed person that I really am. I never want Tom to pick up any negative vibes from me and so I brace myself again before going in to the ward. It all feels so unreal. I am like a clown with so many masks in place. It is hard enough for me to deal with his reality, without trying to fully acknowledge the depth of my own pain as we journey together. The more I visit, the more I get used to the hospital routine and the different states I find Tom in.

When I brought back his pyjamas I stayed two hours just sitting beside him. He is so relaxed with me, I feel very special. We joked and laughed, then he slept and dozed. He didn't take a drink at all and later I found him very disturbed with the darting pains. I also found the atmosphere more difficult and upsetting. Watching Tom's life fade away is very sad – life not ended, but changed …I experience great calm when I sit with him but sometimes the calm is disturbed by horrendous storms of unbelievable pain. The walk home re-grounds me and gives me time to reflect on what is happening to Tom and to me.[8]

Struggle as I do each time I visit the hospital, I never miss a day and sometimes visit more than once during the day. The greater part

8 Personal Journal, 20 November 1996

of me wants to be anywhere else, but before I know it, I smell the disinfectant and furniture polish and then I'm on my way into the ward. It is a real head/heart battle and the heart keeps winning.

I record in my journal that Tom gives me great peace. But as I look at our journey together thus far, it appears to be anything but peaceful. I look more deeply and begin to recognise the peace and calm in it for both of us. Our communication skills are so tuned now that we are able to exchange glances and nods to minimise talking. The effort of talking, composing sentences and trying to be heard and understood is often too much for Tom. This non-verbal system works well for us, but he uses it to cut off some visitors. I often scold him about this but he simply 'plays dead' or dismisses me with a smile. It is all very amusing to observe the ways he uses his illness to his own benefit.

I have occasion to bring someone to visit who Tom doesn't want to see. When he spots her, he tenses up, joins his hands as if in prayer, closes his eyes and pretends to be dead. She moves slowly to his bedside and kisses him. She whispers in his ear and prays over him. Through all of this, he does not move a muscle. As I observe the antics, I fight back a chuckle. He is like a bold child lying there. Behind the chuckle, I wonder about a relationship that leads him to choose to play dead, even though very soon that will be a reality. I worry that he might feel totally isolated and alone if he thinks that I have betrayed him by letting the woman visit. I also hope she senses that he doesn't want her around, and that she won't volunteer to come again. Since I don't understand their history, I have to trust that it will work out. Part of me expects him to be grateful for visitors, which is putting the visitor's needs before his.

When this visit ends, I take the woman for a cup of tea. We talk about Tom and how unwell he is. She has travelled some distance to be with him and it is extremely upsetting for her that he isn't welcoming at all, that he shuts her out. She realises that her presence is very upsetting for him and decides that it will be better for both of them if she doesn't call again. I am relieved that she sees this and that she doesn't have to be told not to come again.

Before we leave the hospital, I make an excuse to call back to the ward and check on Tom. He isn't happy with the visit and I apologise for bringing her in. I also explain how impossible it would be not to bring her, or worse still, wonder at the prospect of her getting a taxi and confronting him alone. We clear the air quickly and actually laugh over her intrusion. He does, however, extract a pledge from me that I will do whatever I can to prevent her from coming back. This is a big pledge to keep, but I say I will talk with her and do my best. I try to convey to him that her visit is her decision – not his and certainly not mine.

When I meet her again in the foyer of the hospital, she agrees to fly home and probably not return until the funeral. This is a frightening prospect for her and for me. I grow nervous of the ever-decreasing numbers of visitors coming to Tom. I feel I am on the 'front line' of a battle of wits between Tom and some of his visitors, and I wonder how many will continue visiting when he keeps cutting them off. I know that Tom needs support in his illness and he is getting a lot of support from an ever-diminishing group of close friends, but I selfishly ask who will be of support to us on the 'front line' of this journey. I am finding this a cold and lonely place.

Tom is in need of care and comfort and respect for his space and his time. I can give him the care, comfort and respect for the moment and he now trusts me. He will talk to me a little. We have had such honest exchanges about the cancer and his current situation. This afternoon has left me gutted. There is such sadness that they cannot be together at this time. Her presence implies his death is imminent. His rejection leaves unclosed issues for her – too sad for words. I found myself fighting back the tears as I tried to tell her not to come back. I can understand him wanting someone like me to continue visiting because we don't have a history – I am part of the present and even though we have been through bad and sad times, these times are recent and they haven't had time to fester or upset him deep inside.[9]

I am aware of the limited time Tom has, but I still want to be able to fix his sickness. A miracle cure would be wonderful, but I know it won't happen. I begin to understand how the strain, pain and fears around a terminally ill person can lead someone to consider euthanasia. I know I often wish I could take over and end this sickness. Knowing that the time left is short I start to question the reason for putting a person through so much in order to keep them technically alive. On a daily basis, I watch Tom's life ebb away until he is only a shell of his former self. The person I now visit is a far cry from the person I knew a few months ago. Despite my tiredness and my desire to end my part in this journey, I fight the negative thoughts that sometimes nag so relentlessly at me.

Tom does not have children, but he does have relatives and through them I hear that he will be transferred to a home very soon. The notion of transferring him makes me shiver, but I know I have to trust. One afternoon Tom has a visitor and, when she leaves, he maintains that he doesn't know her and that she must be lost. I make it my business to find the same woman and I ask her who she is. She says she is the social worker and she reluctantly tells me that she has just told Tom that he is moving soon. I ask her if he understands what she has told him and she says yes.

I go back to the ward and it is very clear to me that Tom has no understanding about what the social worker has told him. He still maintains that she was lost and visited by mistake. He has no

9 Personal Journal, 20 November 1996

idea of what has been said about moving. In order to prepare him for the move, I tell him that I am looking out for a better place for him to go to – one where people won't be roaming in and out of the rooms uninvited. He smiles at the idea and I'm not sure if he is smiling at my innocence, or laughing at my stupidity for not realising he actually does know exactly who she is and what is going on. He knows though, that if I say I will look for a better place, then I more than likely have a place in mind. The break comes when the hospital is informed that a bed is available. The hospital agrees that I can travel with Tom in the ambulance and a date and time for the departure is arranged.

A few days later at noon, I phone Tom's friend Simon to say that I will travel with Tom in the ambulance and Simon agrees to collect me once Tom is settled in. With all the arrangements made, I leave and take time for myself to come to terms with the transition that lies ahead. I decide to stroll up to the hospital in time for the noon departure, but a strange feeling comes over me much earlier in the morning. I go with my instinct and run to the hospital to find that the ambulance is already parked out front.

I make my way to the ward and find the staff transferring Tom onto the trolley. He is struggling against the move and resisting the ambulance staff with all his energy. His arms are flaying in the air as if he is drowning in the moment. Our eyes connect and I signal to him to settle down and not to worry. I don't say anything in particular, but simply gesture with my own hands that he is to calm down. I stay with him and the ambulance staff successfully transfers him to the trolley. Meanwhile, the nurse packs his personal belongings into his suitcase and a few plastic bags. Tom doesn't take his eyes off me for a second. The other patients in the ward glance at me quickly and then turn away. I want them to say something but I know if they do, I'll burst out crying. I watch Tom being wheeled away to the lift with some of his plastic bags sitting on the trolley beside him. I take his suitcase and walk alongside as far as the elevator. There is not enough room for me in the elevator so I walk down the stairs. I am consumed by my own emotions and inner turmoil.

Tom has grown to trust me so much and now, I feel like Judas selling him short. I know and understand the prognosis and I know and understand that we must move him. I don't understand why he and I have become so close – who chose me for this journey? As I ask the question, I think of Newman's meditation – "GOD HAS CREATED ME TO DO HIM SOME DEFINITE SERVICE; HE COMMITTED SOME WORK TO ME WHICH HE HAS NOT COMMITTED TO ANOTHER." Well, I hope I will live up to his faith in me. Judas had his job to do, and now I have this to do.[10]

Tom does not speak at all in the ambulance. He lies on the trolley and stares fixedly at the roof. I spend the four mile journey convincing myself that the move is for the best. We arrive and I gingerly step out of the ambulance with the suitcase in my hand. I walk slowly into the building, staying close to Tom all the time. This building smells of new carpets and everyone smiles as we approach reception. We are brought into a beautiful room and the nurses greet us affectionately. Their kind words of welcome makes us feel so at home, I can hardly believe it. We have landed in 'Never Never Land'. The staff, the atmosphere, and everything in this new place is wonderful.

Unlike the hospital, there appear to be lots of staff available to help us. At one stage I ask them to all leave the room so that Tom and I can find our feet. It is like finding the pot of gold at the end of the rainbow. We both look at each other in disbelief, wondering

10 Personal Journal, 20 November 1996

if this dream will end and we will wake up with Tom back in the hospital. One of the nurses returns to the room to assess Tom. I leave with another nurse and we complete his admittance sheet. I explain that he refuses painkillers and ask whether anything can be done to ease his pain. In no time, the nurses manage to convince him to take the painkillers. For the first time in ages he is able to sit up in a chair and watch television. Visitors can come any time they wish and their visits are easier since he is looking so much more at ease. I feel better about taking breaks from him because there is always someone close by if I need company. My greatest fear has been that Tom will die alone. Well, in this place there is always a friend close by and a listening ear.

I can hardly believe the transformation in Tom. He is looking better and feeling a lot better in himself. As I sit with him, I find myself thinking of the times he would visit the family and all the stories of decades gone by. I'm sad that those days are gone, but it is time to live in the now and in our new reality. I'm glad to be with him even though I hate the circumstances. Tonight, I found the following reading from Isaiah really helped me: 'No need to recall the past, no need to think about what was done before. See I am doing a new deed, even now it comes to light; can you not see it?'[11] *These two lines are a source of great hope and support, even though at the moment I can't see the light – or maybe I can. I don't know. I'm confused. We are in a new place, a new way of being and we are moving forward towards a light. I'm afraid though to look and see the light because it will be the end of this part of my journey with Tom and soon I will have to venture alone into something new and unknown – YET AGAIN.*[12]

---

11 Isaiah 43:18-19

12 Personal Journal, 22 November 1996

I always like to feel I am in control and making all the decisions in my life, but at times like this, I realise that I rarely ever make my own decisions. Situations come up and I respond to them. The response is like the first step into the unknown, and it is taken in faith and trust.

The nurses often speak to me about Tom's progress and his prognosis. They never hide the truth and I must say that I find it easier to deal with the truth when it is spoken with such compassion, care and clarity. This new place gives me a chance to open up to the reality of my own situation too. I see many parallels between Tom's journey to his death and my journey through my eye problems back to health. I see myself needing to let go of so much so that I can face possible surgery and the subsequent healing. I need to face up to the fact that while my health will recover I am no longer the same person who left my job that September afternoon. Being with Tom has changed me for the better.

The staff find him very weak and are not sure of his mental state. I am locked onto an emotional roller coaster with him. The whole affair is very hard sometimes and I'm stuck for words. I am getting more tired and anxious over Tom. I have heard that I am the only one he'll talk to and I am the only link (real link) with the staff. While I should feel very special, and I do, I also feel a massive strain and burden. Daily I pray for the strength to keep going with the 'smiley wiley, happy wappy' face that he is used to seeing. He lights up when I come in to the room and we share serious and sad moments, mixed with childlike banter.[13]

Although Tom's condition stabilises, it is clear that the time left is very short. I have a trip booked to visit some friends for the weekend but I realise I will have to postpone it for the time being.

---

13 Personal Journal, 26 November 1996

The last weekend of each November is reserved for a few of us to meet up, and it is a trip I look forward to, but this year it is not to be. I cancel the air tickets and I phone my friends late one evening. They are also friends of Tom's for many years and are saddened to hear that he is so ill. I tell them that I don't want to leave him while he is this bad and they fully understand.

I really want a break from all the sickness, but I know I can't leave now - I won't leave now. I note in my journal that "I cried as the phone went down. I was convinced he would be dead by now and all would be 'normal' again. What is normal? I'll never know the old days again, too much has happened and is happening. My tears are pure sadness and guilt rolled into one". I convince myself in the early days that I will get used to watching Tom getting sicker and sicker. I think that if my head knows what is happening, I can cope without feeling the feelings. Not true. The reality is that I live each day feeling that I am being torn and pulled in every direction. In my journal I note that "My emotions are still upside down and I don't know how I'll react when he does die. It would have been so easy to go away for the break and come back when it's finished".

Tom still plays dead when he has visitors he doesn't want to talk to. When he recognises an unwelcome visitor, he gets into position and stays completely still for the duration of the visit. It scares the visitors witless because, in their innocence, they assume they have witnessed his last moments. Naturally enough, these visitors rarely stay more than a few minutes. I laugh inside when he does it but I chastise him for being so 'nasty'.

One evening while I am with Tom, a Franciscan friar, wearing his brown habit, calls in. I remember hearing years ago how Tom had a run-in with a Franciscan and, since that encounter, he has held all Franciscans in utter contempt. Tom moves into his 'lying in state' position and the friar smiles. He blesses Tom and then proceeds to have a very long conversation with me. Before long we discover that he spent time on the missions with one of my aunts back in the 1960s and we also discover that he knew my father since 1953. Indeed, my father made him his first suit for his mission work in Africa.

We smile as we watch Tom lie as still as can be, barely breathing and practically going blue, and we continue talking. As soon as the Franciscan leaves the room Tom opens his eyes and looks at me. "Did you hear all that?" I ask him. He pretends not to hear me so I ask him again in a louder voice, "Did you hear all that?" "Yes," he snaps back. "Well," I say, with a broad grin on my face, "from now on he'll probably be calling in to see me and not you, so you needn't be playing dead or you'll end up going completely blue." We both laugh.

I can never be sure how Tom will be at any time and, to my great surprise, I call one afternoon to find him much improved and wanting to go home. He chats coherently and seems to understand everything that is going on. It is wonderful to see him almost pain-free for the few hours and, once he is without the pain, he is open to all sorts of ideas including the prospect of going home. For him to go home, someone would have to do a major spring-clean, but the idea of cleaning up his place, which has been vacant for some time now, does not appeal to me at all.

He looks at me and I smile as I ask him in a real cheeky way, "Do you expect me to go home and clean the flat for you?" He replies "No" and then, quick as lightening, he asks, "Can I go home with you? Will you look after me?" We look at each other intently and I say, "Yes, of course you can, but not until the doctor says you're well enough". This idea of going home with me gives him a bit of a boost for the rest of the day. Later, Tom teases me over a clown I have in my hand. I tell him that I bought it at the Christmas Sale which is taking place in the building. He is aware of the noise and the activity of the people attending the sale and wonders about it. He can't figure out this clown though and as he looks at it, I tell him it is me, the joker in the pack, but also like Shakespeare's clowns, very serious inside. He doesn't argue and I take this to be a sign of approval and also a relief for him – he might have thought I had gone soft and brought it as a gift for him.

Tom starts to deteriorate again and wonderful friends and regular visitors begin to upset him. He knows he is not well and that he is growing so dependent on people for simple things. He is no longer eating anything and needs help when he wants to go to the bathroom. He tries to have some normality by watching films on the television in his room and keeping up to date with the news. Doing this much takes a lot of energy and he gets angry when visitors speak over him while he dozes in the bed, or if they speak while he is trying to watch television. He loves the old musicals and knows most of them by heart, but he hates any noise while they are on. I guess this type of intolerance comes from living alone and having the comfort of volume control and noise control in his space. Besides the issue of noise, Tom's pain is being treated more often which means that his condition is more critical. I know he knows that he is worse and he doesn't want people looking at him as he disintegrates.

I wish it was all over – he has suffered enough. Truth be told, I have suffered enough and I'm finding this very hard to go along with. He barely talks at all and thankfully we are still on the same wavelength, so at least we can make some gestures to each other. He also trusts me so much that I feel I should stay as much as I can. As I sit watching him, I'd not be surprised if he slipped away now. He is very weak and frail and feeling low.[14]

---

14 Personal Journal, 30 November 1996

Sitting with Tom, I want everything to be quiet, but people who come to visit continue to chat and talk about Tom as if he isn't there, or as if he is deaf. All I yearn for is peace and calm, the very attributes I had found when I first started this journey six weeks ago. I, too, grow intolerant of the noise and want to simply sit and be with him. I think I am growing jealous of the others who come to visit.

Tom is still very bad, but alive. I truly did not expect him to survive the night, but he did. The staff are keeping me up to date and we agreed to limit visitors to a minimum. An attempt to relieve an internal blockage failed, so he is very tender. I still don't know how to react. People are really upsetting me because they won't stop talking. I want silence and peace . . . there is now a small pump giving him his morphine which makes a slight swish as he receives the medication...he now only responds when spoken to. The butterflies in my stomach are acting up most of the time and right or wrong, I wish it were all over. I can do no more except sit and hold his hand when he wakes. He is very frightened all the time. The difference over the day is dreadful.[15]

My own routine is in turmoil. I think of the things that I might be doing were I not sitting by Tom's bed. I want to be with my own family, sharing a meal, talking about the things that normally bore me witless. I keep wondering why I have been chosen to be here. A few of us decide to keep vigil during the day and the nurses say they will look after him during the night. They promise to contact me, day or night, when his condition changes. I leave reluctantly and try to get some rest at home. The following day, I return in the morning to find him still distressed. I leave the room while he is attended to and when I return a short time later he looks so unwell I can hardly cope.

---

15 Personal Journal, 1 December 1996

Tom looks dreadful – so bad I burst out crying when I went back into the room. My Franciscan friend found me and simply held me as I sobbed. My eyes have been so heavy, this outburst released some of the tension. Jim has come back and reported that Tom upset him after I left last night with his crying and pleading for help. He said he went to jelly inside and did not know what to do.[16]

I am sad that Tom's friend, Jim, feels so bad, but there is some comfort knowing that I am not the only one having a difficult time with this journey. We all need people with us to help us through our lives. They are great and essential, and I learn so much about myself as Jim and I journey together with Tom, even though at times we get on each other's nerves. Sitting alone with Tom I notice that he looks so pale one could be forgiven for mistaking him for a corpse. He lies still and motionless for hours and the only sign of life is his breathing which is like a haunting hollow sound coming from a deep cavern. I want the noise to stop, but I know when it stops he will be no more. Even so, I feel we have done as St Paul says and "Have fought the good fight, have finished the race, have kept the faith".[17] The time is right for him to go. Of course, this is all to make me feel better. As this stage, I just want to be anywhere else but here. I want my life back.

5pm – All the visitors have now left and the nurse has told me that she believes Tom will wake up. He looks dead, but makes the 'snoring' noise. He hasn't moved in hours. Another staff member drops in. "You're still here," he says. I nod. I don't know why, but something inside refuses to let me go home. My promise to look after Tom, I guess, or maybe being a stubborn mule. My eyes are killing me and I really want this to stop. We've come too far for me to leave

---

16 Personal Journal, 1 December 1996
17 Tim 4:7

now, especially if he does wake up. At this stage the change for the worse has been so obvious that the nurse and I agree the end is close. No one will say how close. It would be nice to know that 'this time tomorrow' or 'this time next week' or 'this time next year', it will be history. I write this because of how I feel and not how he feels.[18]

I wonder as I sit here how Tom might be feeling. Indeed I wonder if he is feeling anything. I am surrounded by and immersed in, my own very palpable and differing emotions. I wonder if he is aware of these and maybe even going through a similar set of emotions. Looking at him, I believe he is a lot calmer than I am and calmer than any of his visitors. What an awful spectacle this must be. Here I am, sitting waiting for the final whistle – a bit like those French Revolution spectators who sat and waited for the guillotine to fall. With all this confusion going on inside me, I know it is time for me to leave and take a break. The night-nurse reassures me once more that she will call me as soon as he gets any worse.

The dreaded phone call comes at 7.15am the following morning. I get to the home by 8.30am. Tom is still alive, but only just. I marvel at his determination to live against all the odds. There is always someone close by, but the closeness does not intrude on my space as I sit quietly. I believe I am writing in my journal all that day, but much more is going on inside my head than I have written down. Long periods pass as I sit and watch him die. I am aware of staff coming and going quietly. Every now and then I can feel the odd tear as it falls on my hand. Sometimes a nurse sits beside me without saying a word. The nurses look after me as I look after Tom. It's like a game of dominoes. I don't want them to see me crying in case they think I am weakening under the pressure and unable to stay the course. As one of the nurses sits with me, she puts her arm

18 Personal Journal, 1 December 1996

around me and I break down. Releasing the burden helps me carry on. It has exactly the opposite effect to the one I expected.

As Tom lies there, still breathing so heavily, I cry inside, asking God, begging God, again and again to "Take this cup from my lips". I no sooner ask, or even demand the removal of the cup than I grab it back and move on. It is a cat and mouse game between my head and heart, and again the heart keeps winning. I pray also for Tom's passage from this world to be an easy passage – easy for him and easy for me.

At the moment, I believe he is unconscious – he certainly feels nothing as staff move him in the bed. The change is so great, it is incomprehensible how he is still alive. I guess it is the 'appliance of science'...I don't mind coming and going from the room, and if he dies while I'm out, it's OK – it's the weeks since Fr John and I called to the apartment that make the difference.[19]

I can only acknowledge the depth of my own feelings in very small doses during the day. I try to be normal, but how can I act 'normal' in this place and space. Again I ask what normal means. I realise more than ever that silence is the best form of communication. A silent look or a glance means more than tomes of empty platitudes. A smile almost reduces me to tears. "Who am I really?" I keep asking myself. As on the previous evening, the noise of Tom's breathing gets to me many times during the day. I want so much for the noise to stop, convincing myself that it will make little difference if it stops in this moment or lingers for another hour or two. I cannot help but wonder why he must go on breathing when his life is, in almost every respect, over. In my tiredness, confusion and the sheer strain of being on this roller-coaster, I turn to watch Tom more closely, looking for him

19 Personal Journal, 2 December 1996

to give me the strength I need to stay put. The breathing goes on and on until 4.50pm. My journal records "In the end, he simply didn't breathe anymore".

During the intervening hours, visitors come and go saying goodbye. One woman comes with roses and makes her peace with him. I don't know if he hears her, but she certainly leaves feeling a lot better. And she is not the only one to have such an experience. I learn that the breathing ends only when the person is ready to go, regardless of how good or bad I might feel sitting there listening to it. The nine hours I spend with Tom that day remain a blur. I remember distinctly, though, noticing the silence in the room and knowing that the moment I had prayed for had come. He is dead. One moment there is life and then the next there is death, as with the blowing out of a candle.

A few of Tom's friends and I gather in the room with staff. I weep openly when I realise what has happened, and then the guilt sets in – my prayers for the noise to stop have been answered. It is over and I hope he is now at peace. One of the woman's roses is placed in Tom's joined hands. I move out to make phone calls to my mother, to Simon and others. I find I can say the words though I can't really comprehend them. Simon asks me to take home Tom's personal belongings and a short time later I leave Tom, taking his small suitcase with me. Again my journal records "I had come in with these [personal effects] and Tom, now I leave with just the personal effects. We had grown extremely close over the few weeks and his departure was difficult".[20]

I arrive at my mother's house carrying his little case of bits and pieces, it is all there is left. A big part of me feels a failure because the miracle cure has not come – I have come home without him. I try to hide the bag from my mother, but she still sees it and

20 Personal Journal, 7 December 1996

starts to cry. I try my best to be strong for her, but I feel too empty and drained of all my reserves. Just when I think the worst of this journey is over, there are arrangements to be made for the public church ceremonies prior to the burial. Fr John and I meet to discuss the readings for the Mass and I feel strong enough to take an active part in the ceremony. I underestimate the effect the weeks have had on me and, in the end, I decide not to take on any active part in the liturgies.

When I see Tom again, he is laid out in the funeral home. He looks much better than when I left him in the nursing home. I am delighted that the undertaker has done such a wonderful job and given him back his smile, now filled with peace. He looks more like the man I had known before the 'day of the body snatchers'. When we arrive at the church I am not prepared for the volume of people. I recognise many of the faces and most know me as 'the girl who had been with him'. It is a funny expression and it conjures up an image of some 'unsavoury' relationship. Of course, given our history, nothing could be further from the truth, but it makes me laugh to think of what might have been the conclusion were this story to have been written as fiction in a television movie. On the contrary, Tom and I share a journey of faith, hope and lots of care and compassion.

During the funeral Mass, I am aware of the people close to me. My mother is sitting beside me and is very upset, but holding back her tears. I, too, am holding back the tears in the hope that I can survive to the end of the ceremony without breaking down. I don't feel I have a right to cry since I'm not connected to Tom by blood. But Tom and I are connected at a deep level, one that I may never truly understand. Jim sits near us and I can hear his breathing change from normal to extremely heavy just before the final blessing and commendation. I am suddenly brought back to reality – Tom is dead. Our journey is over for now, but I know that a new journey is waiting for me. I cry openly as I leave the church, walking behind Tom as he is wheeled out. I recall the time I walked close by Tom as he was wheeled to the elevator in the hospital and it all feels surreal. I am inconsolable, yet I feel a strong sense of peace and calm. I feel extremely privileged to have been chosen for this journey and I know Tom is not far from me.

Tom has helped me so much in his final weeks. I have found a new strength I never knew I had plus a closeness to God I didn't expect. I expected to feel relief when it was over, but at the moment I feel angry and alone…I brought Tom's sister and her son out to meet the staff who cared for Tom. As we walked in the smell of the new carpet met my nostrils and in that moment, I expected to see Tom in his room. The staff talked about how lovely Tom was and how they enjoyed looking after him. People are looking at me and telling me I've great strength. But I'm a crumbling mess inside. I never thought two months ago that I would be in this situation today. I am grateful to God for being able to stay to the end. Something wonderful has happened to me even though I feel rotten. Fr John took my hand as I walked out of the church today – "You're doing great." Yes, I know I'm doing great – but it hurts so much and there are no painkillers for this.[21]

It is less than a week since Tom's death and I am surprised by the strong waves of emotions I feel. I am trying to be normal, trying so hard to do the ordinary things, but I miss visiting Tom. I miss his smiles and his funny ways. I miss him.

I spent a lot of time today lost in my thoughts and going over the last seven weeks. It was a real Easter journey for me. The 'agony in the garden' as I watched and waited. The 'scourging' as Tom underwent

21 Personal Journal, 7 December 1996

painful medical procedures. The 'loyalty' of those who could come. The loyalty of those who could not come but held us close in their hearts and prayed for us. And finally as we came to the end of the journey, the mutual comforting between those of us who remained for the final moments – what was it like for Mary and John to stay to the end at the foot of the Cross? It hurts so much – how do we go on? How did they go on and still believe? Every part of me aches – I can't believe all this has happened in such a short time. I thought I would feel great, feel delighted with myself for being able to stay until the end with Tom. But all I feel is emptiness, a longing to be beside him again, to share a smile, a look, a quick word, feel the presence and comfort we shared. Now I have some understanding of LOSS.[22]

As I reflect on my loss, the question "Death where is your victory?"[23] appears before me. The answer comes in time. The victory is mine. As Tom dies, I find a whole new life in me which I never knew before. He gives me permission to be the better part of me.

---

22 Personal Journal, 7 December 1996
23 1 Cor 15:55

A CUP OF TEA

I am a link in a chain,
a bond of connection between persons[1]

The only thing finer than a cup of tea is a cup of tea shared with a friend, in my opinion. During the long hours with Tom, tea keeps my spirits nourished and my attention focused on the business to hand. Tom could no longer drink tea, but he did not begrudge me my potion. Soon after Tom's death, I return to the home to visit the staff and to say thank you. It all seems so inadequate given the experience, love and care I received there. I feel so at home in this place, it is the only place I feel comfortable expressing how I truly am about the recent journey with Tom. I feel understood and heard, even though I don't fully understand and hear myself.

As time goes by, I am conscious that Christmas is very close and I want to reconnect with friends I haven't had sufficient time for in recent weeks. I am sitting in a city centre teahouse, sharing a pot of tea with a close friend, Tony. I have been so caught up with Tom I hadn't realised how long it has been since we talked properly. He is aware that I have been involved closely with someone who has died. I explain how I came to be with Tom, and as I speak I am aware that my eyes are lighting up. I notice his eyes filling up

---

1 Newman, Cardinal John Henry. *Meditations on Christian Doctrine; Hope in God*, 6 March 1848

as I recall the events. All the apprehension I experienced during the weeks Tom was ill has been transformed into such a positive and good energy. I am almost embarrassed to be experiencing this positive energy. I imagine I should be crying and looking dreadfully forlorn, but I am so pleased that I had the time with him. I am sad, but I am also very aware of how lucky I have been to be permitted by Tom to enter into that very sacred place which was his dying.

The conversation with Tony moves through many different subjects, but each time it comes back to Tom, I feel this same good feeling welling up inside. The turmoil and questioning I went through during those weeks is being replaced with this absolute affirmation. When Tony asks how I kept going, I recall the support of the staff and carers who brought tea whenever I needed it and gave me a safe place to simply be myself. A smile and a chance to chat or talk accompanied every cup of tea. It is a simple recipe, but a hugely effective one. I was in awe of these people who transformed my favourite beverage into an excellent tool for my survival.

As Tony and I talk, I find the truth of this recent journey being revealed for me by his attentive listening. It is as if Tom is directing the conversation through Tony and revealing to me the things I had not understood before. Tony and I talk about the fact that I was free to start the journey, and not only that, I was free enough to see it to its conclusion – free time-wise and free in myself. It was never part of my life's plan to do something like this and I always imagined I would be more inclined to pay for another to take on the burden and pain rather than risk it myself. My circumstances allowed me to take the risk and go with it. Indeed, I acknowledge I was glad to have Tom around to help distract me from by own problems.

We tease my tale out a bit more over yet more tea and as we do, Tony helps me discover the truth within the story I am telling him. A new version of my recent journey is being written for me. He facilitates me seeing a completely different side to this than I had ever thought possible. Even though the whole experience is still raw, there is a new freshness to it now. There is great hope for a life changed and not ended. My life is changed and Tom is only truly dead and gone from my life when I no longer remember him. Both Tom and I continue to journey together although in very different ways.

As we talk on, new images are appearing before my eyes, as if Tony is drawing them on the table we are sitting at. I see images of winter being transformed into spring, the dark nights giving way to the beautiful colours of flowers and blue skies. The importance of what has happened during the short few weeks is a revelation to me. The turmoil, fear and anxiety are dissolving in this moment and I am becoming aware of the link in the chain that Tom is for me, and that I was for him.

I hold on to these images and I try to apply them to my own situation. I may soon have to go into hospital for surgery and the outcome of that surgery will have a huge impact on my career and my life. It is a time when I am unwilling to talk too much to friends or relatives about my own fears and anxieties. I am now cutting people out just as Tom cut people out. I am only talking to a very limited group of people just as Tom limited the people he talked to. I have no sense of the 'body snatchers' taking over my body, but I have a strong sense of a change coming. My first obstacle will be the hospital stay and after that I will have to deal with the outcome, whatever it may be.

Despite my own strong feelings, I feel so alive as Tony and I part. I feel reborn and ready to take on the world. During Advent, the readings in Church bring me the same great hope and I am particularly taken with the words of the prophet Isaiah.

The people who walked in darkness have seen a great light; those who lived in a land of deep darkness – on them light has shone. You have multiplied the nation, you have increased its joy; they rejoice before you as with joy at the harvest, as people exult when dividing plunder. For the yoke of their burden, and the bar across their shoulders, the rod of their oppressor, you have broken as on the day of Midian. For all the boots of the tramping warriors and all the garments rolled in blood shall be burned as fuel for the fire. For a child has been born for us, a son given to us; authority rests upon his shoulders; and he is named Wonderful Counsellor, Mighty God, Everlasting Father, Prince of Peace.[2]

Our conversation seems to have made sense of the burden that I reluctantly carried. To my great surprise, when I get home, my sister presents me with a woodcarving called 'Compassion'. As she gives me the box containing the carving she tells me that the contents of the box represent what she witnessed the night she visited Tom and saw both of us together. The carving is uncomplicated – two people holding each other gently and carefully. I remember that evening when I was with Tom and the way he was with me. I remember being so conscious of the third person in the room and trying so hard to be myself with both of them, to be the person each of them knew, even though we share very different kinds of relationships. I believe my sister and Tom understood that night that I held both of them gently and carefully deep inside, in the part of me that does not need words or outward signs. The carving has a special place in my home and whenever I am feeling low, it reminds me of the inner strength to be found when we call on it.

I often think of the cup of tea with Tony and how he revealed to me the parallels between the journey with Tom and my own

2 Isaiah 9:2-6

circumstances. Although I try to minimise my problems and am reluctant to talk about them, my situation is serious on so many fronts. I grow anxious and fearful about my ability to heal and return to full employment. I recall the rumour about the possibility of blindness and recognise the internal blindness I have had for so long and that Tom taught me something about. I am aware that my sick pay will be halved at the end of the first six months and that it will stop at the end of twelve months. I have no idea how I am to look after myself should I not be in a position to earn enough to cover the bare essentials. I am beginning to see my independence ebb away. For the first time in over fifteen years, I am looking to my family to help me out.

As the months go by, there is less communication from my work colleagues. They are getting on with their lives and I am beginning to feel like an outsider to them. There is a strong sense of 'out of sight, out of mind'. The peace and calm I experienced with Tom is fading and being replaced with the kind of fear and pain I used to see in his face. I find myself unable to talk to old friends and family about how I feel. I'm afraid that if they know how upset I am, they will worry and I don't want them worrying. I am in a state of denial and looking for comfort through keeping busy. I think of the hours I spent with Tom and these memories sustain me through the fear, pain and anxieties. I cling to the power of the silence we shared and the strength to be found in being still.

I wish Tom were here because I believe he understands my predicament. I am in the middle of my silence and fear, and I am unable to talk to old friends and relatives. I want someone to hear my worries and know that they are real. The feelings I am now experiencing are so similar to what Tom went through, even though our problems are very different. It gives me comfort to know that I could be with him and I know that

I will have people to be with me. My challenge now is to be open to receive them in my time of trouble just as Tom received me in his.[3]

The gift that Tom was to me is one that I now want to share with others. I give serious consideration to the idea of seeking some voluntary part-time work experience as a helper in the nursing home. After all, I am sure that my skills with tea-making and dish-washing could be of use somewhere in the organisation! I also know that there will be times when I might swap the kitchen work for some time sitting with the patients. Recalling Luke's Gospel, I can see myself as Martha in the kitchen but also as Mary sitting with the patients.[4]

Today I was reading the parable about the seed growing day and night until the harvest. I think of myself, growing quietly inside and when necessary, coming up with the resources to cope with the problems and difficulties. At the moment the seed is growing – I am growing, and I know I will be able to respond when called to do so.[5]

Before I apply to return to the nursing home, I keep myself busy cleaning up Tom's apartment and sorting out some of his books. I walk into his bedroom to remove the bedclothes for laundering. On the mantelpiece in his bedroom, I notice a small figure of a Franciscan kicking a football, dressed in the football strip of his favourite team. I can't help but smile. I bought it for him many years before when I was on a trip to Assisi. I knew at the time that he had had a row with a Franciscan and had held all Franciscans in contempt since then. I bought it for him just to give him a rise – an act of pure divilment. When I gave it to him he had a glint in his eye as he pretended to be disgusted with me. Suddenly I experience a

---

3 Personal Journal, 21 January 1997
4 Luke 10:38-42
5 Personal Journal, 5 February 1997

rush of great memories and I feel so lucky to have had the time to know Tom a little better. I finish sorting Tom's apartment in early February. Two weeks later I attend a memorial service for Tom and light a special signed candle for him during the ceremony. For the first time in months I meet up with people who were visiting the nursing home at the same time I was there. I have a strong sense of camaraderie with them even though we hardly know each other.

Two days after Tom's memorial service, I get word that my surgery is scheduled for the following day. I pack Tom's candle into my personal effects and make my way to the hospital. I appear to be completely calm, almost totally removed from what is happening. I am checked in and go through the final tests before the surgery itself. When I am alone, the calmness disappears and I am so scared. I have a phobia of doctors and hospitals, and yet I am here trying to be calm. I check the time on my watch and figure that in twenty-four hours, it will all be over. With this and a hundred other time-checks done, I eventually settle down for the night. There are a few visitors, but I am not able for them at all. When they tell me not to worry, I become twice as scared.

The surgery takes place early in the morning and the first thing I remember is hitting one of the nurses as I come out of the anaesthetic. I try to call out but my voice won't come. I want to ask her to get the surgery over with as soon as possible, only to be reassured that it is over and all is fine. I then become aware of the bandage on one eye. Back in the ward, I doze for most of the day. The nurses explain that the two eyes were operated on even though only one eye is bandaged. I am so relieved to hear this. I don't think I could face going through this procedure again had they decided to do one eye at a time.

The following day, I wake up early but cannot open my eyes. After an hour of struggling, I eventually have to ask one of the nurses to come and help me. I can see very little. It is like looking through smudged glass the size of a pinhole. Visitors come and go during the day, and when there is no one around I venture to look in the mirror. It takes me a long time to focus properly. As the image develops before me I burst out crying. The tears flood down my face when I see the state of my swollen and bruised face. It feels like the 'body snatchers' have invaded me, gaining access through my face and particularly through my eyes. It is a horrible feeling as I imagine someone else's hand inside my head. The tears flow for a long time after the revelation in the mirror, releasing fears and anxieties and letting go into something new. Life has changed and thankfully not ended.

I am discharged from hospital within days and return home. I have very limited sight at first and barely see what is directly in front of me. I have to turn my upper body from the waist in order to look to my right or left. Focusing takes so long I have to be careful not to move too fast. I have eye exercises to do each day to improve my peripheral vision. I also decide to re-start my walking routine as soon as I can so that I can feel normal. I forget sometimes that I am bruised about the face and that my eyes are very scarred. It is no surprise that I get odd glances from passers-by.

My first trips out of the house are in very familiar territory with no major roads to cross. Soon I get more adventurous and walk to visit some friends, completely forgetting that there is a main road to cross that does not have a pedestrian crossing. I stop and listen for traffic and step out. I make it halfway and then panic. I go completely blank for a while and cannot see a thing. The cars seem to be driving by so fast on all sides of me. Finally, I make it to the other side, panic-stricken. It's a long time before I go out again without a minder. My eyes, however, improve steadily and I am convinced that I will soon be ready to return to work.

My health worries are abating, but there are still problems regarding my return to the job. My gut is concerned for the future and I am holding on to what Tom taught me – trust. Tom trusted me and I now have to trust others. Neither he nor I saw the true destination we were heading for – I guess I have to keep going not knowing where it will all end. Something wonderful has happened, but I know I am heading into difficult waters in the near future – my gut is usually a good indicator even though I have often ignored it.[6]

Before I know it I have the relevant forms filled out and referees found to support my application as a part-time voluntary helper. The interview follows quickly and within a few months of Tom's death, I am accepted with a start date in the spring. Within nine months of starting the journey with Tom, I am back in the home dispensing tea. I feel I am beginning to bloom again just as the seeds growing in the earth are beginning to sprout. I imagine the seeds growing within me and these are now beginning to bloom in tandem with the seasons. I find myself drawn to some patients more than others and there is no particular pattern to this. I am conscious that each patient is met where they are each day, there is no history between us and we start with a clean sheet. I recall being with Tom and the history we shared and yet we had no real deep history. This is a different situation and these are new relationships with huge potential to grow, or not.

In time I come to realise the importance of each and every one of these relationships. Every person I've met has become a link in the chain which is my life and they form me. They all have lessons for me that only become apparent in time. Just as Tony revealed so much that afternoon as he listened and reflected my own words, the patients reveal other aspects of myself to me in their own way. I am in a very privileged situation each time I meet

6 Personal Journal, 10 March 1997

patients, their families and friends. As with Tom, the passing brings its own sadness, but I am very conscious of the abundant gifts I receive. I am also very aware that there will be many occasions of confusion, fear, sadness and huge turmoil as I decide to freely visit the seriously ill patients. One of my journal entries around this time sums up much of my openness to go forward.

I believe Jesus caused the storm the night Peter walked on water. I believe it was as much a storm inside Peter as a storm on the sea. I feel drawn by something more powerful than myself, to do things and to be in places where I experience storms and upsets, only to reach out and feel upheld and led to safety. I know there will be storms – I know there will be helping hands. More importantly for myself, I feel called to look at the storms inside me – the storms that my gut is warning me about. As my storms flare up, I feel I will be able to reach out for the safe hand that will be there for me. The storms I witness in the people I meet are in a way mirrors for my own storms. It's time to stop looking at the other person – it's time to look a lot closer to home and to my own life. Just as I spent those weeks with Tom and watched his life ebb away, I have a sense that the recent surgery I have come through is the start of an ebbing away in my way of life. I feel drawn into the unknown yet again and this time I know that I will be able to come through even if it is a rough time. Tom has taught me a lot about survival and living through the rough and tumble. My feelings today are something like the ones I had the day I accepted the reality of Tom's mortality and the loss I was about to experience. I wonder if I am being prepared for another loss. Since I didn't lose my fight for health – what am I about to lose and do I really want to know? No, I've had enough to deal with for the moment. Just keep the seeds growing inside me and I look forward to the harvest.[7]

---

7 Personal Journal, 17 May 1997

As I meet the patients I am conscious of how well I am. The success of the surgery is evident and visits to the surgeon are reduced as my eyes continue to steadily improve. I continue my walking and eye exercises. For a short while immediately after the surgery, I have someone remove my car until I am confident enough to drive. Surprisingly, I am back driving within a month of the hospital stay. I am beginning to feel independent again. This extract from John sums up how my journey continues.

Very truly, I tell you, when you were younger, you used to fasten your own belt and go wherever you wished. But when you grow old, you will stretch out your hands, and someone else will fasten a belt around you and take you where you do not wish to go.[8]

---

8 John 21:18

THE EARLY DAYS

There is a time for everything –
a time for tears, a time for laughter[1]

Despite the fact that it only seems a short time between my journey with Tom and my acceptance as a helper in the nursing home, the step to return is not as simple as it sounds. I struggle with the idea of returning to help out, but the draw to go back is bigger than the struggle. When I doubt, I am reminded of the times I used to travel to work with my friend Catherine.

Catherine and I have become good friends over time and we have shared many family upsets in our hours travelling together. Over time she tells me about a friend of hers called Eddie. Eddie is a neighbour who calls in each day to clothe, bathe and feed Catherine's sister, Ann. Ann has succumbed to serious illness and is deteriorating slowly but steadily. As I listen to Catherine talk about him, I am in awe of his bravery. I imagine how difficult it must be to be with a relative who is seriously ill, but I can't imagine opting to be with someone when you don't have to be.

As Catherine tells me about Eddie, I realise how her family could not cope if Eddie were not around. All Catherine's family live a long distance from Ann and can only visit at weekends. Each time they visit, Eddie fills them in on Ann's state of health and the progress of her illness. On Mondays, as we drive to work,

1 Ecclesiastes 3:1,3:3

I have a lump in my throat as I listen to Catherine filling me in on her weekend at home. It is heartbreaking and there are no words of comfort that I can offer. As I journey with Tom, I am not really that conscious of Eddie and his journey with Ann. We seem worlds apart, and yet we are very close. As I begin to see a connection, the draw to the nursing home is much, much bigger than the struggle. I return to the there with both Tom and Eddie as guardian angels.

The cups of tea give me the opportunities to connect with patients. Sometimes I take time to sit with them while they enjoy tea. Sometimes we watch television together. Sometimes we converse and often we sit in silence. The conversations can at first be quite trivial, but there are times when the patients move quickly to a deeper level. I leave the situation to develop or not to develop. I do not plan anything during these visits.

Patients who come from the same part of the city as myself sometimes recognise me and are then more open to sharing stories and anecdotes. I come from a densely populated area with rows of old, terraced houses.

One elderly woman I meet is from the street next to me and we quickly recognise each other. Each day when I arrive at the ward, I call in to see Sheila. She asks after the neighbours and enquires about all the goings-on in the neighbourhood. I fill her in on the latest news and also share stories of times past. Sometimes when her neighbours call, she is delighted to be conversant with most of what has been happening. It is hard enough being so ill, but being far from your neighbours, friends and their lives is a lot to bear on top of that.

Sheila is delighted to be able to keep up with what's happening in her home place through our conversations. She has a sister, Mary, who sometimes travels with me to the nursing home and it's lovely to watch the two elderly women when they meet up.

They are both in their eighties and share a world few have access to. Between them they have a wealth of stories spanning the childhood years they shared in our neighbourhood, followed by the years when they were separated to work in different parts of the country. Neither has married and their family consists of nieces and nephews who live a good distance away. There is a lovely sense of a lost world recalled when they are together. At times I feel like an observer looking in on a history lesson. When they talk about old times, they often mention people I have heard about through the folklore of our area and, on occasion, they happen to include some members of my family without realising it. I have a strong sense that we are supposed to meet and that we are supposed to share our stories.

I cannot help but smile when the ladies have an afternoon tipple as they enjoy some daytime television, usually chat shows with all sorts of topics up for discussion. One afternoon when I call in, the main topic for discussion is sex. The two women look slightly confused as a relatively young person complains fiercely about her sex life. A little embarrassed, I look at Sheila, who simply and quietly says, "Sex – you'd swear it was only invented yesterday!"

As summer develops, I venture to wear one of my skirts while going to the nursing home. When I call in to say hello to Sheila and Mary, one of them admires the skirt saying "I remember when they were in fashion. I had a similar one that I used to wear to the dances". All I can do is laugh. It must be forty or fifty years since she frequented dances.

One of the things I love about the people from my area is their directness and I have been told that I also share this directness when I speak. While Sheila is in the home, there are four other patients from our area there too. Even though I visit all the patients, I find myself spending more time with the people from my own neighbourhood. The nursing home staff often refer to them as 'your people' when they are talking to me. Usually when I call to these patients, I am asked lots of questions about this neighbour or that, about developments in the area and about anything that confirms a link between us. Imagined or real, I feel a special bond with them and I believe they sense that too.

Sheila is well enough to go home for an overnight visit and I call on her a few times in the twenty-four hours she is at home only to find that she is not taking her medication properly. In consultation with the nursing staff, I bring her back. Her health deteriorates a lot over the few hours, but picks up when the staff are again looking after her.

Over the next few weeks, I call on her often and bring her whatever she needs. She talks about a cousin she used to visit when she was a child some sixty-five years earlier. She knew this cousin entered a convent but has no idea where she is now. After some detective work, I locate the cousin and bring her out to visit. It is a lovely reunion for the women and a welcome surprise for Sheila and Mary. Soon after this reunion, Sheila dies peacefully one afternoon.

On another afternoon I bring out a video about the history of our area. In the video, many of the older residents tell stories about growing up during the 1916 Easter Rising and the Emergency. Local characters give very entertaining accounts of life in the inner city. Intentionally or not, this video has the wonderful effect of getting people talking, especially as it evokes numerous memories. The reactions are hilarious as people recognise friends and neighbours on screen talking about their childhood memories of the area. Patients who have nothing to do with our part of town are also intrigued by the stories. The family of one such patient even asks for a loan of the video to bring home. It is amazing how a simple thing like a video opens up all sorts of conversations and draws people from very different backgrounds into the one place and space.

Soap operas too can be great fun to watch with a patient. Often I pass a comment about a television character and the reaction I get back generally tells me something about the patient. With some clarification and more conversation, it is surprising what will be said. Seemingly, I can come across as being quite serious, although this is not my intention.

One day, when a particular low-budget hospital drama is on the television, I make a comment in a very offhand way. "See your woman with the white coat, her hair tied up and the glasses – she'll be transformed into the hospital 'sex symbol' as soon as she removes the coat and glasses and lets her hair down." As I speak, my prediction comes true. The woman I've spoken to, Betty, looks surprised and responds "I bet when you're not here, you're a riot". I take this as a great compliment. My cover is blown and so is hers, because now I know that she too is more than likely to be a riot when she is not here.

I become a regular visitor to her room and we spend time talking about all sorts of things. When her daughters call I excuse myself and leave them to get on with their visit. I believe Betty tells her girls about the conversations we have, particularly the funny ones. As time goes on, I come to realise that she is a native of the inner city too and that she moved to the suburbs when she got married. She is a grandmother, but I only meet her children during my time in the home. I realise that since I have no history with Betty, every time we meet is a time to learn about each other, simple things such as likes and dislikes and, on occasion, some deeper insights come about.

Betty was brought up in a part of the city that is being redeveloped. When we talk about the markets and the street vendors, it is hard for her to hear that apartment blocks and fancy hotels are replacing them. It's hard for me to accept these changes too. Each change brings a little nipping away of the things I know and am accustomed to. It is like the erosion of my history in a way, even though I am very much part of the history being created today. Betty and I talk about the necessity for this growth and see a lot of positive things in it, while we also lament the simplicity of a life that has gone.

I visit Betty often and really enjoy our conversations. She relaxes as we chat about her family and her late husband. She is very proud of all of them and looks forward to their visits. Some evenings I feel tension in the room as Betty's health starts to deteriorate. She grows impatient with her illness and with herself. She is not able for the banter we share, but she is still able to smile when I call in. She has a wonderful glint in her eye when I am joking with her. And I really enjoy teasing her about dropping me just because her own girls have come in to visit. I pretend to be offended that I am no longer wanted once they come.

As the time moves on, her girls spend more time around the bed with moist eyes and they are barely able to smile. I call to the room to see that everyone is alright and offer Betty some tea. Despite being very unwell, she comes back as quick as a light with "Tea for three". In a cheeky way, pretending to be upset, I say I only have to bring tea for her. The girls smile and I go off to get the tea for three. When I bring it back, she has the glint in her eye again, enjoying the fact that she corrected me and told me to bring tea for three – I love that. I love the way she still has her divilment even though she is so poorly. Visitors often feel compelled to walk on eggshells around patients, so it's nice to hand Betty the opportunity to exercise authority, albeit 'pretend authority'. I believe she enjoys these exchanges and the daughters certainly enjoy the space to have a laugh.

Within a very short time, Betty dies. I call out the day she is reposing in the mortuary and ask one of her daughters for permission to see Betty. For the first time, I see her wearing a lady's tweed suit. Up to this, she always wore casual clothes, tracksuits and sports tops. More striking than the tweed suit is the fact that she doesn't have the glint in her eye. Usually when I'd open the door, she'd look over with a smile in both her eyes as well as the smile on her lips.

When I come out of the room, Betty's daughter is smiling at me as she wipes away tears. I tell her that Betty looks well, but explain how I got a surprise when I saw her dressed in the posh suit. I also comment that she looks so serious and I miss the divilment she normally had in her face, particularly in her eyes. Her daughter smiles as she tells me that I was the only one who used to draw this out of her. "She was mad about you, luv. Did you know that? She loved the banter the pair of you had." I have no answer. Fighting back the tears, I sympathise with the remainder of the family and leave.

I am so surprised by the kind words and I reflect often on this short journey, acknowledging that I was and am very fond of Betty. I cannot explain how come the two of us hit it off so well. Every afternoon we could spend so much time talking about many things. She proudly told me about her daughters and their families, about when she was young and her life in suburbia. When her family visit, I feel like I know each of them, even though we are never introduced.

A few weeks following Betty's death, I attend a bereavement service in the home. When Betty's daughter walks in, she bursts out crying when she sees me and her husband tells me that this is the first time she has allowed herself to let go and actually cry. I am battling to maintain my own composure during the ceremony and am relieved to be able to have a cup of tea with her and her husband later in the evening. As we talk, I realise the importance of making real connections with people. Betty and I connected in a way I don't understand, but her daughter can tell me that Betty loved me. This time I can respond with "And I loved her too. She was a very special lady".

Christmas is a hard time for many families, and particularly hard when a member of the family is unwell. I find it can be a difficult time to be with people in such sadness.

It's New Year and I am looking for good things in all that I do, but sometimes, just hidden below the surface is a deep well of sadness – my own sadness. Unexpectedly, I went to the home today – so many are close to death. A very young widow called in. The look on her face haunted me for ages, and I was reminded of how I was when Tom died. To say the least, it was difficult today, yet I am aware of exactly what was going on. There are people going through what I went through, but for each of us, there is a different pace. It is not easy for anyone, but now I don't run from the pain. Now I can listen and share with those in hard times.[2]

Michael is a new man who sometimes needs company when he is having his meals. He follows the daily news stories with great interest. He is aware of a number of news items including the deregulation of the city's taxies. Before this deregulation, license plates for the city's taxies were very expensive leading to what some considered to be a 'closed shop' in the taxi business.

I am asked to sit with Michael while he eats his supper. He has one eye on me and one eye on the television as he contemplates the scrambled egg on his supper plate. I offer him some food and he tries to chat. Michael's conversation is mainly made up of

2 Personal Journal, 23 January 1999

questions and I focus on answering the questions as I offer him his food. It is a delicate operation trying to feed him and I try not to be disrespectful as I endeavour to respond to the questions and not spill the food. I don't mind the questions. In fact, I am amused by them and find myself answering each question as it comes up. Eventually, he asks: "Do you have a plate?" "I do," I answer, conscious of the supper plate in my hand. "You do?" he says, sounding very surprised, "did it cost much?" "No," I answer, "I got a few as presents." He looks at me, stunned. "Presents? They're very good presents, very expensive presents." I start to think about the variety of plates I have at home, some old pottery and some more expensive china plates and I'm curious about his fascination with my crockery.

Suddenly, I glance at the television and notice that the news bulletin on the screen is all about the protest around the deregulation of the taxies. I eventually realise that Michael is talking about taxi licence plates and not my crockery. I continue, "Yes, they were presents, I have a few on the go at a time". He stops asking questions and comments, "You're awful young to have that much, aren't you?" "I'm not that young and it is only a few plates," I say. He finishes his supper, giving me a few unusual glances as he does. I smile at him and when he is finished, I leave the room telling him "I have to go now and wash the plate".

I call in with supper for another man who smiles and asks, "What's your name, Mary?" "Paddy," I answer. "That's strange. How come I can't remember that?" "Well," I respond, "think of whiskey and call me Jameson." "OK Paddy." He never forgets my name from that day and always smiles when he ventures to say 'Paddy'.

Another woman, Sarah, shares my enthusiasm for old movies with suave actors such as Seán Connery and Cary Grant. We particularly like some of the old comical movies where we can enjoy a laugh.

Sarah's illness has left her unable to walk and now, as time goes on, she is losing her ability to talk. She and I communicate using an alphabet card – I point to the letters and Sarah blinks when I point to the next letter she requires to make up her word. It is slow work, but before long I am acquainted with the regular words she needs me to hear. I sometimes laugh inside at the prospect of asking her what she would like me to bring her and for her to start spelling out the likes of *Cosmopolitan* instead of *IT*. Sarah and I grow to trust each other quite quickly and we often share a laugh over the silliest of things.

I call to see her and find that she is getting worse. The alphabet card is not working as well as before and I find it very hard to understand her needs. We rely on eye contact, but now her eyes don't laugh like they used to. They are filled with sadness and fear. Sarah cries when she is alone and I find myself spending most of my afternoons just sitting with her, keeping her company. There are no words shared between us and I am acutely aware of the very real 'sound of silence'. Behind the silence there is a lot more going on, there is trust, compassion and caring between the two of us. We still have some eye contact and at times, she can raise a smile.

Even as I watch her body break down, I know that her mind is perfect and she is fully aware of all that is going on around her. She is able to watch all the activity knowing that she will never again be fully part of it. I cannot imagine what it is like for her to be locked in her body, watching all of us coming and going, and not being able to do or say anything. I don't want to visit her as much because I know that she is getting steadily worse and there is nothing I can do. But that's rubbish. It's not about what I can do. It's about simply being present. What was it You said in the Garden of Gethsemane? "The sorrow in my heart is so great that it almost crushes me. Stay here and keep watch with me." That's it – I don't want to visit because the sorrow in my heart is huge. Also, I'm not sure that I can stay and keep watch with her. No words – just be – that may be too difficult for me.[3]

I call to see Sarah in the hope of being able to 'stay and keep watch with her'. When I call, she is very upset and crying a lot. I ask her if she has pain and she indicates that she does. The nurse gives me painkilling cream and I start gently rubbing her legs and arms. Each time I stop applying the cream, she starts crying again. The tears come slowly and when I look into her eyes, I perceive a longing from her for company. It's as if she is afraid that I will leave as soon as I believe the pain has eased. In my heart I believe I am anointing her in preparation for the final stage in her life. I finally leave after three hours of anointing and gently rubbing her. She is calm and more relaxed and ready for some sleep. I leave knowing that we will not meet again. She is returning to her family home the following day to be with her husband and children.

I walk away a changed person. I may feel drained and in need of someone to anoint me, to make me feel better and give me some energy, but I come away happy that I have fulfilled my journal entry. Yes, I may have managed to 'stay and keep watch', but I know I cried inside when she cried outside, and I felt pain and sadness. I have watched this cruel illness take its toll on her and on her family over the short time we have known each other. She never complains, though. She accepts it and welcomes each day as it comes. She shows gratitude with her smile for the smallest kindness. I look back on our short journey together and the lessons I've learned. She has taught me that I do not need words to fill the gap, silence can be golden. She has taught me the importance of never giving up on someone even when the outlook is bleak. She has taught me not to walk away, but

3 Personal Journal, 17 April 1999

rather to walk in and BE. I leave feeling drained on one hand but filled with gratitude on the other – thanks Sarah.[4]

The early days help me understand that people can come and go from our lives, but life itself goes on. Each introduction is a new birth. There is a period of learning how to communicate effectively. The forming of a relationship that goes beyond the surface often follows this, and finally there are the farewells as people leave again. I learn over time to accept these phases and see how my own life moves through phases. I had only noticed the obvious ones such as the passage through childhood years to school and beyond. Life is filled constantly with new relationships and farewells, what I call 'little births' and 'little deaths'.

I look at nature and the lessons offered to me in silence. Trees grow deep into the soil to find their nourishment and rest in the winter before bursting back into full bloom in spring. Watching myself in the middle of the work I do, I see myself being challenged to dig deep into my own resources and also needing to take time to rest before bursting back into bloom.[5]

My journal entries give me a chance to be myself and to see more clearly the power of what I witness. These early days as a helper are so important for my personal journey which has been difficult recently. I see all the patients as God-given to help me deal with my own health and career challenges. Tom brings me to a point where I can sit quietly and trust. Sheila helps me to reconnect with my neighbours, many of whom I had forgotten while I was busy in a nine-to-five job. Betty shows me that relationships start when people communicate deeply and with fun. Michael teaches me the need for clarification. And, finally, Sarah teaches me the power of

4 Personal Journal, 22 April 1999
5 Personal Journal, 24 April 1999

anointing another and the wealth to be drawn from being totally and utterly present to another in their prison of silence. These are the lessons I record today and I know in time that many more lessons will evolve from these same people as my life moves on. A part of me wants to have them, and many others, still around to offer more lessons, but I know that can't be. Nature once again offers me an answer.

I notice that a tray of seedlings I have is beginning to look cramped and some of the seedlings appear to be squashed and weak. As I separate them and plant them in the garden, they are finding space for healthy growth …so I guess there is time for sticking together and time for letting go to give space to others so that they can find their own strength. This letting go is not easy for me but I have no choice. I am grateful for having had these wonderful times being bunched together and also the space to grow.[6]

---

6 Personal Journal, 24 April 1999

MARK

Come to the water[1]

My favourite part of helping in the nursing home is visiting the patients, getting them their afternoon tea, watching TV with them and sharing stories. It is February and the doctor has just suggested in a casual way that I invite a particular patient out for a drive with me. I am delighted, thrilled with the trust she places in me. As I float down to his room on a cloud of self-satisfaction, I imagine all sorts, thinking of where we might go and what we might do. I open the door and the vision before me is certainly not part of my image. This man, Mark, looks so angry and serious I am sure we will never get on. I smile and close the door without exchanging more than a very brief "Hi". I tell myself that there is no way I can take this man out today. And I don't. I find lots of other things to do and then go home at the end of my shift.

I think of Mark often and regret not making a better effort on our first encounter. Two weeks later I spot Mark sitting in the foyer. He is dressed in his day clothes and looks a little happier. I venture to offer to take him out for a spin in my car. He immediately says yes and suggests I pick him up at his room in half an hour. I call to his room exactly thirty minutes later and we set off on our journey.

---

1 Isaiah 55:1

I decide to take him to a hotel about three miles away where we might watch an international rugby match on the big screen TV in the company of regular people. Before leaving his room I help him put his leather jacket on. His jacket is like a huge heavy bag and looks like it might weigh more than the owner does. Mark is at least twelve inches taller than myself and he towers over me. He is also extremely thin. My attempt to help him with this jacket is fruitless – in addition to it being too heavy to lift, I can't reach up to put it firmly on his shoulders. As we walk out together, I am very conscious of how different we are in appearance. His height and lack of body weight contrast my low stature and round features. As Mark towers over me, I feel like a tiny bug being led away by a giant. I'm not sure though if he is the friendly gentle giant or someone else. I do know that we look a most unusual pair, very like the characters in the children's poem about Jack Sprat and his wife Kate.[2]

I open the car door and again, Mark's height is a problem for my little hatchback car. I push the passenger seat back as far as it can go and he loads himself in. It takes him quite a while to get into the car, manoeuvring himself slowly and cautiously until he is fully positioned in the passenger seat. We're off!

There is little or no conversation until we arrive at the hotel. We get out and stroll slowly into the main reception area. All heads turn to look at us and I do everything I can to act normal. Mark and I find a table in the lounge with a view of the TV and I am tempted to stick my tongue out at all those who stare, but restrain myself with great difficulty. Conversation is lukewarm, but he tells me he is pleased to be out and about. He finds himself restricted

---

2 *Jack Sprat and his wife Kate / ate their dinner from one big plate. / That was funny I declare / but then they were a funny pair / Jack Sprat could eat no fat / His wife could eat no lean / And so, between the two, / they licked the platter clean.* (Nursery Rhyme)

within the complex of the home and although he can come and go, he does need a driver such as myself to bring him out and look after him. It is hard to tell if he likes the hotel, but I think he is absorbing all he can from this venture out into the 'real world'.

I am pleased with how we get on and I am willing to take a longer trip on another occasion. While our conversation is minimal, silence is not a strain between us as we both enjoy people-watching. It doesn't take long to realise that Mark is a very direct speaker which suits me well and once we say what is bothering us and, of course, what is pleasing us, we both get on fine. This is just a short first trip to whet his appetite and when we go back, Mark is very happy to have the option of going out again. So far in our brief relationship, I have made all the decisions, so I ask him if he would like to choose the destination for our next venture.

I am so pleased that Mark and I went out today. I was thinking over the two weeks about the parable of the two sons [Mt 21:28], and feeling rather disappointed with myself that I said I would take him out and then didn't. I am delighted I got the second chance to do as I had said I would, and more surprising than that is the fact that we got on so well. His angry face does not reflect accurately the person he is. He has a depth he does not easily share – I look forward to our next outing.[3]

A few days later, I call in to see Mark and find out where he would like to go to next. I am willing to attempt a full day-trip on the following Saturday and invite him to choose a destination within thirty miles. Barely moving his head to look at me, he simply says "Newgrange". Newgrange is a five-thousand-years-old passage grave and is one of my favourite places to visit. From the outside it looks like a small hill or mound of earth. For me it

3 Personal Journal, 7 March 1998

is a symbol of both eternity and mortality. I am curious about his choice but say nothing at this point. I leave Mark and make my way home looking forward to the trip he has chosen. I am a little apprehensive too, since this is going to be a lot more adventurous than a trip to the local hotel to watch some rugby.

Saturday arrives and I call for Mark. He is ready and waiting. We have all the medication and the necessary advice from the nursing staff. It takes just a short while to load up and we set off for Newgrange. The roads are fairly winding and unpredictable and, for the first time, I am conscious of how painful these roads must be for someone as ill as Mark. He doesn't complain at all about them, but he does talk about the wonderful countryside and the green fields and forests.

It is early spring and everywhere is coming to life after the winter hibernation. I notice Mark is also coming to life despite the advanced stage of his illness. He may be physically weak, but his spirit is strong and indeed strengthens as he reconnects with the natural world around him. He soaks up the energy from everything that is alive, but he doesn't deplete the energy source. I watch and learn, intrigued by his way of being.

Driving along, we share stories about the mountains, forests, sky and cosmos, and their interconnection with our own lives. Mark talks about creation and the fact that it is outside of our control or design. "You know we come into the world with nothing, Paddy, and we leave with nothing. It's up to us to do the best with what we have in the meantime, but we can't take any of it with us. We are here for a reason and we are all interconnected even though we may not realise it at the time," he tells me.

Indeed, he does not think it is an accident that we met or that we are on this day-trip. He sees us all as being part of a much bigger plan. His views and the simplicity of his words stun me.

I really enjoy listening to him and being part of his world. Neither of us talk about our families or our personal relationships. Mark talks a lot about himself and his place in the world. Everything for him has a purpose and at this stage in his life, he is winding down and preparing to return to his source. In time, I understand from him that his source is God and that this is his unique and very personal journey back to God.

When we arrive at Newgrange, he appears to be disappointed. He expects us to pull up outside the ancient site but instead I pull up in the car park for the visitors' centre. Everything here is very new and he cannot see anything that is five-years-old, let alone five-thousand-years-old.

We walk slowly down to the entrance of the centre and he is delighted to hear the sound of the River Boyne rolling alongside and quietly comments "Ain't nothing softer than water, but it has the power to erode rocks". The smell of the trees and shrubs attract his attention too and once again, he is grounded in creation and is at peace. He catches sight of birds making nests using the foliage and twigs which litter the path we are on. The sight of each of these miracles of nature halts him in his stride. In a very exact way, he moves his body to face each of the things that attract his attention.

As I look on, Mark looks like a human camera, photographing as much as he can see and hear for his eternity. He adds little or no commentary. He simply looks and listens attentively – maybe he is giving thanks for being permitted to be part of it all. I know I certainly am.

Before we look at any of the exhibits in the visitors' centre, we have a cup of tea and decide how we will approach our visit to the site. Mark is very tired and weak and he tells me that "The disease is taking over every part of my body". He decides he will not be well enough to look at anything and wonders about getting a refund. As he looks out the window to the mound on the other side of the river, he is convinced he will not be strong enough to walk over. I am disappointed for him and suggest he rest a while before doing anything else.

He continues to gaze out the window taking in the view. As he looks at the river, he suddenly realises he can't hear it anymore. The strong windows and the noise of people going about their business block the gushing noise. "I can't hear the river, but look at how it moves down over the stones, eating them away, just like my illness is eating away at me," he says. All I can do is nod my head in agreement. It is the truth and even though we can't hear the wearing down, it is happening all the time. He sees that as being the way for all of us. I ask him to stay put while I go to the staff about getting permission to drive up to the mound.

The staff accept my word that he is too unwell to visit the mound in the normal way and refund him his admission fee without question. They also phone over to the guides at the mound to tell them that we will be arriving under our own steam. I am moved by their sensitivity and Mark is delighted to have his refund. We stroll back to the car at our slow and exact pace. Once again we soak up the nature around us and then make the short journey to the mound by car.

Mark gets out of the car and takes a deep breath. Here we are at one of the most splendid sites in Ireland, a site that houses five-thousand-years of our history. I am nervous, though, about the fact that this is a passage grave, and wonder why Mark has chosen this place for his day trip. He leads the way to the entrance and the guides welcome us and invite us to take our time. Mark walks towards the entrance of the passage grave but doesn't go too far. He suddenly stops and looks all around. Trying to hide my nervousness, I give a history of the mound and the other passage graves in the area. I mention that we are standing close to one of the small pots that might have housed the cremated remains of one of our ancestors. I am cautious though about mentioning anything about death or dying and yet it is impossible to avoid the subject since this is a burial ground.

I stop when I realise that Mark is once again lost in the world of creation. He admires the Boyne Valley, the hills, the greenness of it all and then tells me "Soon I will return to the soil and become part of all this. Then I will fertilise the new growth and new life". The very notion of being part of this wonderful creation fills him with a huge sense of purpose. His life will be fulfilled through his death.

As the seasons come and go, I see myself moving through life – the seasons come and bring plants through their life, they come and bring me through my life. Some plants bloom annually, others bloom and return to the earth and die. As Mark talks about the closeness of his death and the closeness of his gods, I see our lives as being nothing but short stories in the greater scheme of things.[4]

Mark is happy to have been on the hill and he enjoys the life all around him. I do not ask him if he wants to go into the passage grave and we move back to the car without entering it. Mark generally makes it quite clear when he wants something in particular, but at this point I imagine he thinks about his own passage grave that is being prepared as we admire the scenery, so there is no need to go in, not yet anyway. It is early in the day still and he is keen to continue sightseeing.

Our next port of call is Tara, the ancient seat of the High Kings of Ireland. We enjoy more history and still more connections with ancestors and the eternal cycle of life and death. The history of Newgrange and Tara is a history of struggle for power and

4 Personal Journal, 14 March 1998

kingship, and a struggle for faith. Mark can relate to the struggles and sees his illness and his time in the nursing home as a similar struggle. His faith is strong. I am not sure where he might see the power and kingship in his life at present. He is surprisingly open, however, to talking about what is happening to him, which is so refreshing. It is a privilege to be part of his life at this difficult stage for him. His journey is giving both of us life, against all the odds. I find it hard to believe we only know each other a few days. Mark refuses, however, to go back to the home, so we drive as far as the city centre. After a brief drive through one of the city parks, he once again refuses to go home.

I normally attend my own parish church for Mass at 6pm on Saturday and I invite Mark to join me there. This invitation is entirely for myself as I really need some quiet space for myself after all the comings and goings of the day. Mark reminds me that he may not be well enough to stay at the Mass so we make a deal. I agree to sit near the back of the church and in the event of his getting ill, I agree to take him back to the car. He reluctantly agrees reminding me again that he isn't feeling well.

Once again we endure the surprised looks and stares of the people. I make my way to the back of the church and find a comfortable seat with lots of legroom for Mark to stretch out. He settles in and actually enjoys the Mass. I am so delighted to have found a quiet space for myself at the end of a very long day. It is customary to share a handshake, a sign of peace, during Mass and I am moved by the strength of his handshake and the eye contact we make. I truly do wish him all the peace he can find for the final days of his earthly life. I am oblivious to the other people in church until I hear "God help her" coming from the row behind us as one caring woman spots Mark when he turns to shake her hand. The priest, a good friend of mine, also does a double-take when he sees us walking up the aisle for communion. As he gives me communion he says "the Body of Christ, are you alright love?" "Amen. Yes I am, Father," I say.

We return to our seats smiling. I am sure Mark is listening and smiling at the comments he hears around us. I have a sense of the people being sad for us but also a strong sense of their care and concern. I also have a sense that Mark is enjoying the attention, enjoying the comments and enjoying my acute embarrassment.

At the end of the Mass, Mark agrees to go home after some light refreshments. It is like bargaining with a child and I think both of us enjoy playing the game. He really does not want to go back until the very last minute. My heart is breaking as I eventually drop him off. The nursing staff are astonished at all we have done and Mark is surprisingly energised by all of the different parts of our day together. I am tired though. I'm also delighted that I took the initial step to take him out that second day. I drive home thinking about all I would have missed out on had I stuck with my first impression of him.

The strength I got yesterday from Mark, as he allowed me spend seven hours with him travelling around the countryside, was beyond my dreams. Being with Mark reminds me of my need to stay connected with family, friends, my surroundings and with God – it gives me great hope for our futures. As I listened to Mark, I learned new ways of dealing with fear and upsets. I notice that he focuses on nature when his pain is very bad. He also talks openly about his impending death, seeing his journey to death rather like the road to Calvary. He says that Jesus did this for him and now he does it for Jesus. Where is his anger? I think I am angrier than he is – and this is his death.[5]

I am so aware that Mark is not expected to live longer than a few weeks. How many weeks, it is impossible to say, but his time is

5 Personal Journal, 14 March 1998

short. I decide to make the most of the time we have and plan to do as many things together as we can. He is delighted when I suggest we go out again the following week on St Patrick's Day.

As I get to know Mark, I seek out venues for us to visit which are filled with nature, but which also have ample places for him to rest up. Our next outing on St Patrick's Day takes us to Newbridge House. This is a large stately home with fine grounds. We decide not to take a tour of the house and once again our first port of call is to the coffee shop for fuel. The coffee shop window looks out onto the farmyard where there are many fine pieces of old farm machinery on display. We marvel at the lifestyle of our ancestors as we watch adults and children enjoying the equipment.

Mark and I are not inclined to stay indoors or to stroll among the exhibits in the farmyard. We set off instead to the gardens, in particular the wooded area. We walk slowly along a short path lined with evergreens. The ground is carpeted with the spines and cones from the evergreens and as we walk on the carpet, the smell of pine comes up to meet us. I've often walked quickly along this path without noticing a whole lot, but today, it feels so luxurious.

Mark and I don't talk very much. He stops mid-step and takes a deep breath. He is soaking up his surroundings again. Looking at me, he gently says, "Thanks for taking me to this place". I know nothing of Mark's past, but I imagine forests and evergreens have a special place in it. He looks so at home here, I decide to linger as for long as he wants. We even find a bench to sit down a while and absorb even more of this place. I wonder about all the millions of people throughout the world who are rushing around to catch a Patrick's Day parade and here we are, delighted to be surrounded by trees, nature's carpet and its wonderful smell.

Mark tells me that he loves a particular Thai restaurant in the city. He doesn't know the name of the place but he lists off landmarks close to it. I book a table for us in the restaurant closest to the landmarks he describes. Of course, I book the wrong place and, of course, he insists we go to the one he meant.

When we arrive in the city, I leave Mark for a moment so I can phone the first restaurant and cancel the reservation. As we walk down the busy city streets the crowd parts and everyone seems to stare at us. I have grown so accustomed to Mark's unusual walk and gait I no longer notice it, but not with all these people. I am uncomfortable with their insensitivity and I break the silence with the question "Are they looking at you or at me?" His reply is quick and exact, "I rather think they are looking at the two of us". He is right – 'Jack Sprat and his wife Kate' out on the town again! I smile and keep going.

When we arrive at the restaurant, I am surprised that the owners know him. We are shown to our table and Mark orders his favourite dish for himself. This is my first time in a Thai restaurant in my hometown so I decide to order just a starter. Since I am not that adventurous when it comes to matters of the palate, I suggest that we share everything. Mark teaches me about the different types of dishes and the different flavours. I eat whatever he leaves behind and he smiles as he notes that "For a little person, you can certainly pack it in". I keep thinking of the rhyme I had learned in school years before:

Jack Sprat and his wife Kate
Ate their dinner from one big plate;
That is funny I declare,
But then they were a funny pair.[6]

I find Mark intriguing and am surprised by how much I enjoy his company. I know by the look on his face that he is enjoying my

6 Nursery rhyme

company too as well as our adventures. My first impression was so negative but our trips are full of fun, with lots of space for us to be serious as well.

We decide to venture out again, back to our original 'haunt', the hotel with the large TV. This time, we totally ignore the people who stare and enjoy an hour at the coast away from it all. We are quiet, both of us observing the people around us. Mark's pain is getting worse and he finds it more difficult each day to carry the weight of his jacket.

I know I only know Mark for a very short while, but already we have grown quite close. It hurts me to see him deteriorate so much – the pain is now more etched on his face. He looks thinner and he finds it difficult to walk. The car is so small and it takes a lot more effort for him to get in and out. I find our trips great, but they are difficult for me. I believe he enjoys them but is it becoming very painful to visit the world outside, knowing that he has fewer and fewer chances to do so. I imagine he looks at everything as if it is the last time he will see it. Is he seeing his mortality staring back at him?[7]

Mark loves Thai food so much, I decide to risk another trip back to the same restaurant. He is delighted and I arrange to call and collect him on a Tuesday evening. My phone number is available to the staff in the event of Mark needing to change plans. I get a phone call telling me that someone is expected out to visit Mark and he cannot come out to dinner. The weather is dreadful, so it is a blessing that he can't come. I am concerned that he might get a chill that would wipe him out completely. I am also disappointed at the prospect of missing our meal together so I arrange for a take-away from the same restaurant and collect it as soon as I can. The restaurant waiter recognises me and asks after Mark: "How's your friend, he

7 Personal Journal, 17 March 1998

not good tonight?" I am surprised that he remembers us and am moved by his concern and compassion. People are wonderful.

Food in hand, I make my way out to Mark. I open the door to his room and he looks so sad. His expected visitors have yet to arrive and he is not too happy that their visit meant the rearrangement of our plans. I unpack our feast and his face lights up. I pass on the kind regards of the waiter and the pair of us tuck in. His face is a picture as he makes his way through the satay and other delights. The smell of the food floats through the corridor and there is a stream of 'jealous' staff coming and going from the room checking out what we are eating. The final visitor can hardly hold back the comments as he smirks and even laughs at us. When he opens the door, he finds me putting all the evidence of the meal in the rubbish bin - like bold children at the end of a forbidden midnight feast. I leave and Mark sees me off with a huge smile and heartfelt thanks. We are like the cats that got the cream.

I am so pleased that I got the take-away tonight. He sounded irritated earlier when he phoned about not being able to come out, but the look on his face when I arrived with the bag of goodies was worth a million dollars. I think he plans his time around our trips and missing one upsets the schedule. So far, I am managing to contain my emotions. I find myself, however, getting quite close and almost entering similar territory to the one I had with Tom. Words aren't as important as being present and available. The head and heart are playing games with me again. The head says I don't need to do something – the heart says it would be good for us to do it – the heart keeps winning out. The heart is steering me again, and I am afraid that the heart is bringing me into tempestuous waters once more. Truth be told, I am enjoying Mark so much – I know it is going to be harder with time.[8]

8 Personal Journal, 24 March 1998

Mark tells me he has a visitor coming from overseas and we decide to take her to our Thai restaurant. I'm quite excited about meeting his friend and making a link with his former life. I still know little or nothing about Mark. All we share is very much to do with his current situation and his illness. I look forward to the meal and make the arrangements to call out on the following Wednesday evening. The staff are delighted with Mark's progress and our busy social diary is now a joke among them. Mark and I don't mind their teasing. The fact is we're having too much fun to care about it and, truth be told, we actually enjoy the ribbing we are getting.

I call out on Wednesday as arranged and as soon as I walk into the home one of the staff asks what happened to me on the previous evening. It turns out that Mark got the night wrong and was ready and waiting at 7pm on Tuesday instead of Wednesday. I call to the room and he looks over at me – "I knew I must have been wrong when five past seven came and you weren't here," he says.

He and Laurie, his visitor from overseas, are praying when I walk in, and neither is free to come to dinner on this occasion. They ate earlier and only later wondered if I was due out today. I stay a while and then leave them alone to catch up on their news. Mark is so disappointed with himself for making the mistake and I'm disappointed to have missed the chance to meet Laurie properly over a lovely meal. I want to say there is plenty of time for going out but of course, that is just not true. We postpone until Friday, just two days away.

He looks so intense sitting praying with Laurie, as if every bit of energy and concentration he has are necessary to keep going. They obviously are very in tune with each other and I sense there is a great pain, which comes with long-term friendships. I can't imagine her pain as she sits with Mark, facing his dilemma with him. I think now how I felt the first time I sat silently with a dying person – there is nothing else to do but sit. I think of how much easier it is for me to come and go from his room – but it is not really that easy for me at all. I'm just a big softy at heart and I know I will grieve deeply when he departs. Why oh why do I do this? I don't know.[9]

I call for Mark and Laurie a little later than originally arranged. I phone in advance to let them know I am running late in case they think they have the evening wrong again. I am glad we are in the city on a Friday night so that Mark can see the place alive with all the weekend revellers. He is much weaker now and getting to the restaurant is a slow process. As we pass one of the American-style diners en route to our Thai restaurant, he smiles at the noise of the music and people inside. Our restaurant is very close by, but is a much more sedate and quiet place. Our table is upstairs, which is less noisy than the main floor, giving us a good opportunity to talk and get to know each other better.

I enjoy listening to Laurie sharing stories about herself and her ventures. I am learning about Mark, too, and his time in North America where he worked for many years. This explains his Irish American twang that becomes more American than Irish while Laurie is visiting. Mark and I share so much and yet we know so little about each other. During this dinner, I discover that he has family across the Atlantic. As we share a great meal, we share ourselves on one of those rare occasions when there is only room for reality, whether that reality is very serious or very funny. I really enjoy these occasions when there is no role playing on anyone's part – everyone is being themselves in a genuine 'what you see is what you get' manner, take us or leave us, we don't mind and we don't apologise.

---

9 Personal Journal, 1 April 1998

Laurie is staying in a guesthouse close by the home and I drop her off on my way. She is so strong during the meal but when the two of us are alone, she breaks down. She is heartbroken watching her friend deteriorating before her eyes. He is much worse than the last time she saw him and this time when she goes back to North America, she knows she won't be visiting again. She is wondering what it is that is keeping him alive. He has already outlived the doctor's original predictions, but she wonders how much longer he will survive.

My heart goes out to Laurie who has travelled thousands of miles to say goodbye to Mark. She wants to be with him when he dies. I know that feeling so well. She also tells me she has just a limited time here. She doesn't want him to die, he is still a young man, but she knows he is going to die. Because she lives thousands of miles away, she really wants Mark to die while she is visiting so that she can go to the funeral. I find this peculiar talk at first, but now as I reflect, I cannot conceive of not being able to hop in the car and drive to a funeral to say goodbye. So much of what I experienced during my time with Tom is coming back now. It is like reliving my own journey, as I journey with Mark (and Laurie). But this is different as well. I am the outsider to a large extent and yet Mark is very free with me. I feel sometimes that I am intruding in a place that Laurie used to be. I don't envy her situation at all. I cannot imagine the pain of having to board a plane leaving her friend behind so close to death. Whatever and however this unfolds, I know I will stay the pace. I did it once before – BUT it is NO easier the second time.[10]

I am very good at putting the different parts of my life into neat pigeon-holes. This means that I can be totally present to Mark and

---

10 Personal Journal, 3 April 1998

Laurie while I am with them, even though my health and career problems are ongoing. My surgery is deemed a success, but there is a new problem that needs to be investigated. I have been suffering from severe headaches for three months since my surgery and the doctors are concerned about these. I put them down to the worry about my 'real' work and career, so I decide to take a break for myself while Laurie is visiting.

Just before I leave for the weekend away, I get word that I have to have a brain scan. I try to joke about the scan being needed to ascertain if I have a brain or not, but behind the jokes, I am very worried. Being with people who are so seriously ill sometimes leaves me thinking the worst when it comes to my own health. Naturally, my headache is automatically a brain tumour to me. The more obvious solution is that one of the stitches has not dissolved properly and that this is causing my headaches.

Even though I enjoy the break very much, I often think of Mark and wonder how he is getting on. I also think of the uncertainty about my own future and wonder how I am getting on. Before I know it, the few short days are gone and I am back home. Easter is almost upon us and I am finding that so many parts of my life are breaking up before me. There is a big shift from that day with Mark in Newgrange when I could see so much in a clear and nature-filled way. Now, despite the lovely break, I am home to poor health, personal and career uncertainty, and the imminent death of Mark. I love what I do, but I confess that this is not easy.

I try to enter into the Easter journey as told in the Scriptures, but I am as lonely and as frightened as any of his followers were two thousand years ago. I am consumed by my losses and cannot see anything good – was it like this for Mary Magdalene at the tomb? Am I open to hearing myself being called by name? NO. I am growing so used to being afraid. Is this the new me? Surely there must be something else – is there another person coming into being? How much lower am I to go before I reach the bottom of the pit and start to rise again? I am watching myself breaking up on a daily basis – it's like Tom's description of the 'body-snatchers' when he was dying of the cancer. Mark is much worse too. He is descending into his pit and preparing to start over in a place where the living don't have a role. Learn from Mark – adopt his way of seeing the positive side by looking at nature.[11]

My journal reflects a very sad and difficult time for me. There were many things happening outside of my journey with Mark and I do not see the connections. I try so hard to separate all the different strands of my life, but here I am with a great teacher, not seeing or hearing his lessons that will help to bring the strands together and heal what is broken. I am ashamed of my lack of faith and my blindness. I have all the hopes and the desires to believe, but falter when challenged.

I often think of what Jesus said to Peter, "I tell you, Peter, the cock will not crow this day until you have denied three times that you know me".[12] Well, inside of me I can hear a cock crowing. I am thinking of the last day with Tom and wondering why and how come Mark is still alive. I wonder about his visitors and expect someone very special to turn up before he can let go. I sometimes think Laurie must be this person, and if she is, I wonder will he release himself while she is with him?

What is Mark hanging on for? There must be someone coming that he wants to see. Maybe he is waiting for Easter, which is only around the corner. He is so strong in his beliefs; I would not be surprised

---

11 Personal Journal, April 1998

12 Luke 22:34

if he releases himself on Easter morning. I'll have to wait and see. That is one of the hard things about all this – the waiting and the not wanting to wait.[13]

Mark is determined to do as much as he can, but I think he tires himself out in the process. He sleeps most of the time with Laurie sitting close by him. She looks anxious and tired, not knowing the hour or the day that the inevitable will happen. She looks longingly as I enter the room, hoping for some change, but we both know it is not going to happen.

I am so relieved that Mark has Laurie visiting. She and he go back a long way and they can share the stories that mean absolutely nothing to me. Laurie's being around means I can take a back seat for a few days and re-charge my own batteries for the final part of the journey. I feel so sad these days. Are our day trips and little outings a good idea? Am I fooling myself and Mark into thinking that they have a purpose? Am I the only one to benefit from them? How long is this tunnel we are travelling in and where is the light at the end of it?[14]

I am smiling publically while holding back my anxieties about Mark, but I am afraid. Easter is approaching and the similarities between Mark's current state of health and the road to Calvary are striking. It is getting harder and harder for me to stay on the road, but I find comfort in the Easter story and in the strength to be found through support from the unexpected.

It is Holy Thursday and Laurie has gone home. Mark is not well at all and our only venture out is to the guesthouse to look after the bill for Laurie. I dread to think what it was like for him saying goodbye to her. They will keep in touch by phone, I'm sure, but being on the end of a phone-line is not the same as being together in person.

---

13 Personal Journal, 3 April 1998
14 Personal Journal, 3 April 1998

I don't know what to say to him, so I say nothing. He tells me that more visitors are coming from overseas and I discover that he has daughters. His younger daughter will be over with her mother. I am amazed that we talk very often at a deep spiritual level, yet he never talks about his flesh and blood. He is anxious for me to meet 'the girls' as he calls them, so we decide to take them for a drive to some of the nice spots nearby. His eyes light up (as much as they can) and I leave him to prepare for the next set of visitors.

I phone Mark on Good Friday and the girls are with him. On Saturday I call to see him and to meet his visitors. We enjoy a cup of tea together and arrange to go out on Easter Sunday. The girls have heard of our escapades and are looking forward to being part of one of them. Mark and I need to find somewhere close by with a place to walk and a nice venue for refreshments.

Easter Sunday is a beautiful sunny day, full of new life and great hope. I arrive at 1.30pm as arranged and Mark smiles at my punctuality. I am so predictable, almost like a clockwork toy. It may make him smile, but for me, I don't believe there is any room for making arrangements and breaking them or turning up late.

We load up the car and drive just a few miles so that the girls can have a walk near the sea. Mark and I remain in the car. It is sunny, but too cold for us to sit out. I am conscious of the silence between us, particularly as he watches his daughters take their walk.

I decide to drive to a nearby hotel for our afternoon tea. It is a castle situated on the side of a hill, completely out of view of the main roads and overlooking the sea. There are wonderful rambling gardens and we have tea in the conservatory which provides great heat and comfort. Conversation is easy and centres mostly around Mark's younger daughter. We don't stay out too long because it is now difficult for him to keep going without a nap. The girls decide to have an Italian dinner by themselves later in the evening. I sense Mark's disappointment at not being invited to join them, so I invite him to have an Italian meal in the city centre with me.

When we arrive at the restaurant, we are lucky to get a table quickly. Mark looks very unwell, but is hugely determined. The walk to the restaurant from the car park is short, but for him it is arduous. I notice a huge difference in him with each passing day. My surprise is that he is still alive at this stage. We buy one meal between the two of us and he hardly eats at all.

As we eat from one big plate, I am close to tears watching him struggle to keep the food down. I want to rescue the situation, but how can I interfere? This is his choice. He needs so much to act and maybe even feel like a healthy human being. We both know he is far from healthy, but we both want to be accepted in the world of the healthy. I know people are uncomfortable seeing us trying to have our meal, but I decide that these are their problems and try, and do, carry on.

I have such admiration for Mark's way of living to the last and I am so pleased he trusts me enough to allow me to be with him. As we leave to get the car, he says he can't walk anymore and he tells me to get the car for him. I have a quick word with the waiter and he leaves a chair aside for Mark to sit on while I dash back for the car. It is perfectly obvious that Mark is very sick and I know that waiter said a prayer that I would come back quickly in case he dies on the doorstep. As I glance back, the sad sight of Mark sitting in the porch of this lovely restaurant is no advertisement for the excellent food we shared. I match the waiter's prayer with a dozen of my own and return as soon as I can.

Again I say I cannot understand how Mark is still alive. What is driving him so hard? I thought he would release himself at Easter, but here we are sharing an Italian meal in the city. Where are you leading us God? I believe we are on the right track, but where oh where are you leading us? I feel such a strong connection with Mark. I accept there must be more to this journey than my commitment to my work here. He is here to teach me about myself – isn't he?[15]

While Mark has his girls, I cut back on my visits and stay connected to Mark using brief phone calls. As with Laurie, I use their visits so I can pull back and allow some space for my own emotions to emerge. Something inside tells me he won't release himself until all these important visitors are safely back in their own homes far away. I know he doesn't like them watching him die, and I also know they have a desire to be with him at this critical time.

When I call a few days later, Mark wants to go out again. It is a warm day and I take him to a different coastal town. It is flat and suitable for walking, but he can't walk anymore. We head off to the castle where we took the girls and enjoy afternoon tea. They have gone home and Mark seems relieved, but sad also. He coped very well with the two sets of visitors and now he has to concentrate on himself.

When we get home, he takes a long time to get out of the car. He is so much weaker now, but still reluctant to accept assistance. As we walk back to his room, he asks me to hold his hand to support him. For the first time since we started taking these trips, Mark is acknowledging that he is no longer able to get about without help. I move closer to him and discreetly take his hand in mine, holding him tight to my side. As we walk slowly and closely together, this very tall man leans gently over me and I try to take the weight and strain both physically and emotionally. He is so stubborn he won't use a wheelchair – that would be like giving

15 Personal Journal, 12 April 1998

up and he certainly is not giving up yet. I admire his spirit and what I see as his strength of character. In this week after Easter, there is an air of resurrection and life, but as I hold his hand, I feel disintegration and death.

On Sunday, I phone Mark and then call out to see him in the late afternoon. When I arrive he looks very pale and frightened. "I committed a mortal sin," he tells me. I am shocked and venture to ask him how. "I missed Mass this morning," he says. I assume he was too unwell to go to Mass but it transpires that he was watching Mass on the internal system and fell asleep. He also tells me that he is frightened about dying. "That's okay," I say, "it's hard to concentrate when the Mass is so remote." "It's not okay he protests, "I woke up and saw a white figure at the end of the bed. I was afraid. I thought I was dead and I was afraid. It's a sin to be afraid; it shows a lack of faith."

I listen intently and allow him to explain further. "The white figure I mistook for an angel was in fact the chaplain dressed in the Easter vestments. He woke me when he opened the door. He only came so that I could have Communion."

As Mark talks, I can hear the fear in his voice. It must be so hard for him knowing that he is so close to death and yet, in that moment, consumed by fear. He is having a crisis of conscience over the fright he got. His faith, or indeed the faith he aspires to, dictates to him that he must never be afraid, but must put his faith in God. To do otherwise implies that his faith is weak and insubstantial.

Stunned at his logic, even though it is plausible, I ask him if he knows which Sunday it is. This, I tell him is 'Upper Room Sunday'. He looks curiously at me and I continue, "It is the Sunday when the first disciples sat terrified in the upper room and if they are allowed to be frightened, even terrified, then there is loads of room for us to have our fears and anxieties".

He looks at me, thinks about it for a while and then smiles. After a short pause he laughs at me and eventually agrees. He tells me again, later in the afternoon, that he really was frightened when he saw the chaplain at the end of the bed.

We talk some more about the Easter story, the disciples and our journey. We sit a while, chatting with the TV switched on in the background, returning every now and then to our fears and paralleling our fears with the fears of the disciples. Mark, I believe, thinks of Judas as the only disciple who ever strayed, but I tell him how I believe there had to be a Judas in order to fulfil the Scriptures. I also remark how grateful I am that it was Judas, and not Mark or I, who had to take on the role he had thrust on him. I believe we are all born to do on earth what we have to do.

I tell him that I often reflect on the Scriptures, particularly the Book of Wisdom and also Psalm 139, and delight in the fact I was known before there were hills, mountains or streams. This appeals to Mark and his love of nature, but he is not entirely convinced that it is all right to be a believer and to be afraid. We have to agree to differ.

Mark settles after a while but his breathing is very bad. It takes him a long time to get his sentences out. As I sit by the bed, the phone rings and it is Laurie phoning long distance. He has a short, difficult conversation with her, which is broken up by fits of coughing. He gives me the phone when he has to cough and Laurie cries when she asks me to look after him for her. I want to cry myself but I hold back my tears for fear of upsetting Mark as well. They say goodbye to each other and the two of us distract ourselves by watching the TV in silence.

My heart is straining and pounding very hard. My chest feels like it will burst under the pressure. I can barely look at Mark. I would gladly swap places with Laurie rather than have her go through the pain of not being able to keep vigil with her friend. I only know Mark five or so weeks and she knows him for decades. I feel like an intruder in their special friendship and I have a sense of how cruel a blow it must be to Laurie not to be able to be with Mark, but I know there must be a reason for this. Time will tell.

Mark and I start to look at a documentary on TV. It is about a senior citizen attempting to be the first person over sixty-five to reach the summit of Everest. As the climber ascends the mountain with his helpers, his breathing changes into gasping. The air becomes so thin as he climbs that he has to assess each day's journey before setting out from their camp. The TV climber has the choice to pull out, something Mark doesn't have.

As we watch him struggle in the ascent, Mark's breathing begins to change until it is in tandem with the climber on the TV. Mark likens his journey at this stage in his illness to the climber's journey to the top of Everest. We smile at the similarity and watch as the climber decides he can't go on. He doesn't believe his lungs will cope with the pressure and Mark stops and looks at me. We both know that Mark can't pull out.

Mark gasps and tells me he can't stop now and when he gets to the top of his mountain, Jesus will be there. I nod in agreement and then he tells me it won't be long. All I can say is "I know Mark, I know it won't be long". I fight back my tears as I try to take my leave. He calls me back though and asks me to wait a while longer. Each time I attempt to go Mark makes an excuse for me to stay. I eventually leave, exhausted and totally drained. It was an extremely difficult, yet marvellous day for both of us.

I share my faith and trust with Mark and he is teaching me so much. Every moment with him is filled with trust, hope and belief in the future. Even though his future on earth is short, he is leading me to better things. This is why we met – isn't it? I leave him feeling drained, but enriched by all that is said between us. We listen to each other and look out for each other. I am told he would have died before now were it not for our trips out together. I am beginning to understand that it is not always necessary to fix that which is broken, sometimes we have to allow the broken to remain broken and to respect that brokenness.[16]

As I leave Mark, he gives me a strong double handshake rather like the sign of peace we shared weeks before at the Mass in my parish. From that visit, he stops people calling, including me, and relies on the staff for all his care. When I phone each day I send him my regards and offer to visit, but he wants "no visitors". I reluctantly and sadly agree. I am upset by the 'no visitors' instruction, and then I realise that I too have issued a 'no visitors' instruction to many of my friends since my own problems started almost two years ago. I don't feel comfortable with friends around watching me go through a rough patch.

I learnt today that Mark is still alive but that it is a matter of hours for him. I realise now that the double handshake he gave me on Sunday was indeed GOODBYE. While at first I was saddened that Mark didn't want visitors, I now understand how he wants to be alone and at peace. I have no doubt it is what I would want, and indeed see similarities with the way I deal with my own difficulties at present. It is a lot easier for me to have 'new friends' around than the 'old' ones – not so easy on the friends I guess. It is five weeks or so since we first went out, and I've watched Mark get closer and more trusting with me. It has been a great privilege to be so big a part of a person's final weeks. However privileged it is, I still feel saddened by his departing, and feel an emptiness as the final hours go on. I accept I provided good company

16 Personal Journal, 19 April 1998

for Mark, and indeed the day he first smiled at me, I knew I'd cracked it. What is always hard is, knowing that the only way out for him is death. And that is one thing we all have to do alone, but each time I journey with someone it is difficult and unpredictable. Attachments are formed and death brings with it a huge empty space. In time this space is refilled with good things and I become more alive in myself as the feelings well up inside. It is difficult and wonderful – it doesn't come any other way.[17]

At first I am not too upset at not being able to visit but, as the week goes on, I grow more anxious and inclined to call out without getting permission from him. I phone at least once each day, my heart thumping at the prospect of hearing the dreaded news. I send my regards to Mark via one of the carers and I find it very hard to respect his request to have no visitors. In conversation with the staff, it is agreed that it might be good for both Mark and I to meet again.

I agree to call out on the following day, but say I'll phone before lunchtime so that there will time to check with Mark that it will be okay with him for me to visit. When I phone no one is available to take the call since all the staff are busy with patients. I phone back a short while later to find out that the staff were attending to Mark who had died as I was phoning at 1pm. I feel cold and numb.

Mark is dead – the battle is over. I heard he was peaceful in the end. I am finding it hard knowing I was so close and yet I haven't seen him for a few days. I need to say goodbye. I also wanted to be able to be there with him for Laurie.[18]

I don't know how to react to Mark's death. On the one hand, I want to cry, but my tears will not come, and on the other hand, I

---

17 Personal Journal, 22 April 1998
18 Personal Journal, 24 April 1998

don't feel I can cry until I see him again. Shortly after his death, he is removed to his hometown, which I discover is a distance from the city. My need to say goodbye is so strong I set out for his hometown and find him in the chapel of repose. In the final days we shared together, I watched him change so much that in the end he was a shadow of his former self. When I last saw him, we watched the climber on TV fail to reach the summit of Everest. Mark has reached his summit, the one he calls Heaven.

I travel out to the funeral home on Saturday afternoon, and find Mark looking very peaceful. He looks more peaceful than I have ever seen him and he has a smile on his face. I smile back and quietly say goodbye. I relax a little and take part in the short ceremony that follows. The ceremony takes place at the time I am normally at Mass in my own parish and I am reminded of the wonderful day we spent in Newgrange and Tara and how we finished the day with Mass among my neighbours and friends. Before very long, I am on the road back home, accepting in my heart that he has gone.

I said goodbye to Mark today. My heart was sick and lonely as I drove out. I had to go though. I had to see him for the last time. This was my pilgrimage and I had to do it alone. Saying goodbye was easier than I expected and I was glad to have been part of the final departure. I dreaded this day and now it is over. It's the first time I've seen his eyes closed and relaxed. I cannot help but wonder why the two of us got on so well and why we were chosen to journey together – time will tell.[19]

On Sunday, a friend who missed me the previous evening at Mass makes it her business to meet me and sympathise with me over the loss of my friend. I look at her as she takes my hand and

19 Personal Journal, 24 April 1998

I allow myself to cry at last. I didn't think anyone would understand that I suffered a loss as well as those who had known Mark all their lives. I knew him only a short time, but I know my life will never be the same again. Having let go and cried, I am surprised at the intensity of my feelings. I honestly hadn't expected it. And now, when I hear of people climbing mountains, pushing their bodies to the extreme, I think of Mark and his summit.

SPRING IS IN THE AIR

Even though they die, they live[1]

Spring is in the air and I see so much growth all around me. Mark may be gone but he has left me a wonderful legacy. Now I see so much more than ever before. In the walls of old derelict buildings, colourful and welcome flowers appear. Window boxes and hanging baskets of flowers are being hung on the small terraced houses throughout the inner city. The balconies on the apartment blocks are beginning to show signs of spring too. Landscaped gardens are bursting with an effusion of colour and new life.

The way Mark soaked up creation and the beauty of nature spurs me on to spend more time attending to my flowers, watching them come to life as they are nourished and watered. I sometimes miss watering a plant and notice it wilt until it is looked after again. I am at a stage where I feel I am wilting as a result of a lack of my own nourishment. There is a part of me that knows how nourished I am by Tom, Mark and all of the people I have met in my time. But a larger part of me recognises that my health problems have left me wilting and in great need.

As I grieve for Mark, I grow aware of the deeper grief within me for the health and well-being I feel I am losing. I have a strong

---

1 John 11:25

sense of my need to take time out to find water and nourishment for inner growth. Friends tell me I look dreadful even though I believe I am doing a great job of hiding how I really am.

Word comes to say that my scan is clear and I start to think positively again. With the news of an all-clear, I start to look with envy at all of the people living in my neighbourhood who get up each day, dress in their suits and head off to work. I want to be able to do that again. I want to be able to arm myself in my work clothes and head off purposefully and with a confident attitude, like the old days. Just as Mark needed to go out for dinner to feel like a regular member of the human race, I yearn to feel like a regular member of the working population. I miss the old days so much. I grieve for them in a very real way. But I hide this grief behind the grief I have for Mark. I don't think anyone can understand how I really feel. I don't understand how I feel myself but I'd love to be able to articulate what is going on inside.

As the seeds are beginning to burst into colour, it is hard to imagine how such an innocuous thing as a seed could provide such beauty. And that is how it is going to be for me. When the time is right, the colour and bloom will return. It doesn't stop me thinking with considerable jealousy about the woman at the well and how she was heard and cared for during the time she shared with Jesus. I long for my time at the well to come and for me to feel free to speak of what is in my heart and for me to know that I am fully heard. No amount of money could pay for a gift such as this. For the moment though, I continue to plod along in the knowledge that my time will come.

On the one hand I don't understand what is happening to me and, on the other hand, God is sending me great people to hold my hand and bring me along and He is sending me to hold the hands of others.

One big circle of people working together without realising it . . . And the great gift arrived. I got my chance to be at the well and release all the upset. I felt at times that I was at the bottom of the well in total darkness and isolation, but in fact I was being gently held in the light and being heard. The outpouring and the tears leave me drained physically and mentally. I appreciate the power of someone listening without needing to tell me how to solve the problems – no platitudes, no empty words. Time filled with listening and being heard.[2]

The struggle I had with Mark and the uncertainty about how we got on so well is coming back to me now. As Mark, and Tom before him, let go and allowed me to walk with them, I now reluctantly hand over. My health is unsure, my career remains in the balance and my income is all but gone.

God, when the rich young man wanted to follow you, you told him to sell everything he had and give the proceeds to the poor and then follow you. Well, I didn't ask what I had to do to follow you, yet I have lost everything. I have no proceeds to give away. What do you want of me? Am I doing what you want now, or are there more surprises around the corner? Don't answer. I don't think I want to know. The flowers in my small yard are blooming for the second summer in this phase of my life. One of these days I will bloom and I will be sure that the tide has turned and someone has at last turned the light on in the tunnel I feel trapped in.[3]

Great hopes abound that there is light at the end of my tunnel, throwing me once more into a terrible state of fear. All the questions about 'what next?' come up again and again, and I am almost too afraid of accepting the challenge of move on. I think of

---

2 Personal Journal, 30 April 1998
3 Personal Journal, 30 April 1998

Bartimaeus, the blind beggar, who cries out to Jesus to help him. I sense I am whispering for help, still not quite ready to cry it out as Bartimaeus did. I envy him as he accepts the invitation to go to Jesus and long for the day I will throw off my cloak and spring into action.

I am terrified to look too closely at Bartimaeus. His courage is astounding to me. After all he has a steady income from the begging – why give it up? Most people know him as blind – I know what that is like. They know him to have a stick, a bowl and a cloak – these being the tools for his trade. I think of these as being more like security blankets – very little is expected of him while he is willing to hold on to these. When I do risk taking a look at Bartimaeus, I see challenges for me. I feel challenged to risk calling out, risk accepting the inevitable invitation, risk naming what I want, risk throwing away the tools that hold me back, locking me in my current problems, risk accepting healing and a chance to walk away. It's a lot of risks on the one hand, but I am so aware that even if I don't cry out and ask now, the opportunity will keep presenting itself until I see beyond where I am and then decide. I think it's time to revisit the Book of Wisdom and Psalm 139 – God will I ever learn?[4]

Spring gives way to autumn and before long Christmas is upon me. I continue as a helper in the nursing home and I also spend some time in a centre for homeless people. In there, I am surrounded by people who are the modern day equivalents of Bartimaeus. They beg all day and come to the centre for a breakfast and a lunch. I quickly recognise the very thin line between my life and theirs. I am still waiting for my personal difficulties and career problems to be resolved and in time my body's defences run down very low. The constant state of high alert as I wait for word about returning

---

4 Personal Journal, 20 June 1998

to work depletes my own resources so that I cannot fight any illness coming at me. I succumb to pneumonia and only manage to join the family for three hours on Christmas Day before having to return to bed. I feel my body crumble under the pressure. I see it as a further erosion of my former self. It is as if the weaver of my life is changing the pattern of the cloth.

I spend more and more time at the homeless centre and see the parallels between my life and the lives of those who come to be fed each day. I see so many sad and broken bodies, locked in addictions, prostitution and crime, afraid to look forward. I wonder at the ways I am locked in my world and my way of being. I am locked in a world of fear and anxiety about myself. I wonder if I am growing more and more addicted to the status of the job, career and health. Whatever is going on for me at this time, I recognise that I am moving in a new world, a world I had not known up to two and a half years ago and now I am growing more and more afraid to look forward. We are not so different at all, but I notice that some of the homeless I meet make much better eye contact than many of the people I meet who have homes, jobs and an apparently comfortable, stable lifestyle.

The homeless centre is alive with people who are not afraid to display who they are. I was not prepared for the depth that many of them can go to and the sheer honesty they have about their lives. Their spirit and ability to speak about themselves puts me to shame and highlights how often I run from the reality of my own situation. In my head I reason out all that is happening, but these people speak from their hearts. I think I know about how to 'be still and know', but in truth, I cannot 'be still and know' without the fear of really getting to know myself in my heart.[5]

---

5 Personal Journal, 27 March 1999

Another Easter comes and I have yet to experience my resurrection. I feel I know the agony in the garden and Mary at the tomb weeping, but my resurrection eludes me. I feel lost and alone, even though I seek God in everything around me.

My heart is broken and my faith is being pushed to the edge, yet I cannot go through a day without acknowledging that God is with me. Help me to know that when I touch your cloak, you will heal my pain and lead me on.[6]

I am beginning to see His hand in my difficulties as well as in the great things. This is a huge step forward for me and signals a new beginning after the long dark period. I feel I am still in the early stages, but I am never alone even though I may be physically alone. I look at my friends who have died after long illnesses and see the parallels between their lives and deaths and the journey I am on. I look at the homeless and see other parallels with my life. It's like watching my life being played out before my eyes and not recognising myself in it, and truth be told, not willing to recognise myself in it. It is good, however, to know that there is something fresh for me at hand. I know serenity will truly come when I release the fears, anxieties, anger and all that goes with them.

I welcome the new spring and look forward to the new blooms, new colour and freshness and new life for me. Recalling again the story of Bartimaeus, I reflect more deeply on the things that might be holding me back and leaving me feeling locked in and imprisoned. I know that I will feel the release only when I recognise the things that are holding me back. These are the things that hold me in the dark tunnel and prevent me from being fully alive. Once I recognise them, I know I'll be cured of my inner blindness. And so, at this time, I reflect a lot on the job

6 Personal Journal, 5 April 1999

and career I long for. I spend so much time pushing and fighting to return to work, I fail to see all the other opportunities that are being presented to me. I recall being told that I would never be anything other than a computer professional, but after all that has happened, I know I am a lot more than a computer professional. It is a part of me but not all of me.

Finally, and very reluctantly, the lesson sinks in and I release myself from the lovely job I have held as a precious and essential part of me. I decide to stop fighting to return to my career and to put that part of my being to one side. The decision is met with surprise and it takes some considerable time for the paperwork around my decision to be finalised.

Once my decision is enacted, I decide to work on myself to alleviate the stress of the recent years and allow new opportunities to present themselves in their own time. As I put it aside, I tell myself that I don't want nor do I need the career anymore, and that I am ready to start over. And so, I start to live a new life. In a very real way I experience my own death after almost three years of uncertainty, fear, anxiety and illness matched with faith, hope and belief in the power and support of the people around me.

The time I spend in the nursing home and in the homeless centre reveals so much to me, it is clear that this apparent death is actually a new birth and my resurrection. I celebrate my decision with a gathering of friends, both old and new. It's a bit like a wake and a christening party all rolled into one. I am now happy to let the old life go. I am happy to move on with all that has happened and know that I have survived so much heartache to come to this point. I know that I will be able to survive many difficult times ahead with all I have gleaned from this stage of my life.

Opportunities I never dreamed of are being presented to me and I feel absolutely free. Just like Bartimaeus, I have thrown away my cloak and the other tools I thought were essential for me to live. Now, at last, I am coming alive again, both inside and outside. Within weeks I accept an invitation to train as an Anam Chara. This excerpt from the vision statement for Anamcharadas really reflects my life in recent years and also explains the ministry I am undertaking.

"We believe that, throughout history, God spoke through many prophets and most fully in the person of Jesus. We believe that God speaks to us in all our life experience, revealing who God is and who we are. We recognise that, at the heart of each person there is a longing, which is a reflection of God's own passionate longing to be with us. Our longing moves us to make the search for God, following Jesus and living in the Spirit, the heart of our personal collective history." [7]

I laugh to myself at the way God always gets his own way. I am very slow sometimes to recognise what is happening to me and there again, this phase of my own journey is like a whirlwind. Somewhere deep inside me, I know that I was being drawn back to the city centre to live and work with the people there. I know I also needed the experience of my work and career, and the challenge it brought. I could not do many of the things I now enjoy without that training ground. No experience I have ever had has been a waste. I may not have liked some of the experiences but I am sure there is a reason for all of them. Just as Jesus had to suffer and die in order for us to experience the Resurrection, I have had to 'suffer' many problems in order to die to them and experience a resurrection of my own in this life. It is a very nice feeling now that I see the light in the tunnel, even though I know there will be plenty of dark times in the future.

---

7 Anamcharadas Vision Statement, 1999

In recent years I often thought of the parable of the gardener giving the fig tree one more year to bear fruit or he would cut it down. He feeds the tree loads of manure and explains that this is necessary for growth. I fully recognise that I experienced inner growth through all the trouble I had and can now acknowledge the benefits. Anthony de Mello remarked "keep me up to my neck in manure Lord, but don't make waves!" I am recognising the importance of the manure in order to promote the growth. I just don't like the smell or discomfort necessary for growing.[8]

My heroine in the Gospels for as long as I can remember is Mary Magdalene. She is always billed as a woman with a dubious past, but, dubious past or not, she is a loyal friend to Jesus and his followers, right to the end. She faces reality and walks with it. She stays the course when others run. When she cries at the tomb, she takes a second look at the empty space looking for answers. She just never gives up. Her patience and her search for truth pay off and she finds her 'teacher'. I find my teacher in the pain of living through these years. I find my teacher in the simple and the complex. I find my teacher in the people who come in and out of my life; some journey with me for a short time then leave, others still journey with me. I find my teacher in everything. I see the light in the tunnel and I strive daily to move closer to it. I slip back down the tunnel every now and then, but I have comfort in knowing that the light is always there.

---

8 Personal Journal, 11 December 1999

NATALIE

I came that they may have life,
and have it abundantly.[1]

Living in the heart of the city, it is easy to spot the commuters who come to work each day and return to their homes each night, leaving behind the residents who often exist unnoticed in the midst of all the business. My terraced house is close to the city markets, the main shopping streets and all levels of the business, legal and financial sectors. All this, and lots more, is within walking distance of my hall door. Each morning it takes me just five minutes to walk to work. But for many of the other people who come to work in this area, their journey is considerably longer and a lot more stressful. These are our 'day trippers' who live in suburbia and work in the city.

Sometimes, the increase in stress levels in the area is tangible. I smile as I look at everyone rushing hither and thither and wonder what it is all for. We have suffered under the myth of the Celtic Tiger, a myth that encourages the belief that money is god. With this new way of thinking comes the belief that human beings are purchasable and disposable. Others value people with the same criteria they use to value a car or a house or a loaf of bread.

I have to concentrate and reflect a lot so that I don't fall into the trap of putting money on a pedestal and making it the source

1 John 10:10

of my life. I have learned in recent years that the greatest source of my life is the people I come in contact with. With each one of them, I see my God more clearly and more closely. When my area empties of the 'day trippers' each evening, the evidence of homelessness, alcoholism and drug addiction is apparent. There are many shelters, homes and special centres in my part of town to help care for the homeless and victims of addictions.

A friend of mine took up the directorship of a day centre very close to my house. It is hard for him to find people to help out at the weekends and he asks me to help with some kitchen work. I agree, but insist that I'm not happy to be seen in the main dining area. The only mandate of this centre is to feed the homeless and, to that end, breakfast is served each morning and a substantial lunch each afternoon. The centre cares for, on average, three hundred men, women and children at each of these sittings. With numbers like this, there are lots of pots, pans, plates, cups and cutlery to be washed, so the work in the kitchen keeps me very busy.

I start work on the first Saturday, washing pots – loads of pots! I can hear the buzz of the people in the dining hall and the occasional raised voice. There are all sorts of comings and goings and I try to catch a glimpse of some of the people as they take their meals. They don't fit my picture of the homeless at all. They are all ages, both men and women. Many are beaten up, tired and drunk, high on drugs or simply lost and alone. The city is a cruel place when you don't fit into a neat box and none of these seem to have a box to fit into.

I bury my head and my thoughts in the task of pot washing and try not to think about what is happening in the dining hall. This is such a different place to the nursing home, but in both places the 'patients' are sick, in need of care and some are even dying. Some of the day centre clients can be helped and are helped – it is up to them to make the decision to fight the addictions. It is up to us to nourish their bodies so that they can be physically strong enough to meet the challenge.

Weeks pass and I work my way through the kitchen until I am on the frontline serving food. I am no longer afraid. I meet the clients and we exchange smiles, jokes and conversations. Some clients will never make eye contact or say a word while others love to engage. As I serve the meals, I realise how fine a line there is between those of us who work in the day centre and those who seek the help of the day centre. I could so easily be one of them coming each day looking for a hot dinner. I am lucky and very grateful for all the support and help of friends during the difficult times. Unexpectedly, this work is both very therapeutic and very spiritual.

One of our regular clients is an old man with wonderful deep, dark eyes, which can be piercing. When he smiles, his whole face lights up. He doesn't say a lot when he is sober, but can be quite vociferous when he has had a few drinks. Through the years, he has survived the most incredible experiences, including being set alight, robbed, beaten and countless nights living in doorways. Despite our best efforts, he refuses to take advantage of the limited accommodation available and prefers the freedom of sleeping outdoors, even though it leaves him open to more attacks.

One afternoon, when I am chatting with him, he comments on how people say the silliest things to him. He says they are trying to be nice, but their words come out wrong and he ends up being insulted. He smiles and says, "Aren't people strange?" I nod in agreement and think of the times when I've been tongue-tied and ended up saying the most ridiculous things.

Another afternoon, he is fast asleep on the steps outside our church. There is an open day being held in the church and people are coming and going, taking little or no notice of him. In the afternoon, I decide to take a break and make some tea. Soon after I make the tea, he wakes up and begins to move about. When I go over to him, he moves aside as if to get out of my way. Much to his surprise, instead of moving him on, I offer him some tea and fruitcake. He turns around and nods at me. "One teaspoon of sugar isn't it?" I ask. Once again he nods. When I give him the tea and some fruitcake wrapped in a napkin, he walks away from me. Every so often he looks back at me and smiles broadly. I respond with a smile and a wave. When he finishes, he tidies up the cup and napkin and he gives them to me with a word of thanks. These are the only words he has for me in all of this exchange.

It is such a silent world he lives in, particularly when he is sober. This silence can be deafening. Most people in the city go about their business unaware that they are surrounded by others who move about in silence and yet manage to communicate. I come to realise the power of a look, a nod, a simple wave and of course, a smile. Each time I go to the day centre I notice the non-verbal communication more than the verbal communication. Many of the street people, though not all, look straight into my eyes and then speak. They look for someone who will listen before starting to talk. I know little or nothing about the clients and most of our conversations revolve around the meal they are about to eat or have just eaten.

Some clients will begin to trust and then talk a little more. They may mention where they live or how they live. Overall it is very hard to know what exactly they do when they are not in the centre. Some, I know, sit in parks or in doorways or go home to an empty, cold flat. Others spend their time in the city centre begging in order to support their addictions and still others are prostitutes. Of all of these activities, I find the prostitution the most difficult to come to terms with. They are generally very young girls who are forced to work the streets for a variety of reasons. Not one of them actually wants to be on the streets, but they feel locked into this way of life. They can't see any other options for themselves and they are often afraid to even think of a change. I see them going to work in the early afternoon, confident that they will have a few customers before evening. For every one of the prostitutes, there are plenty of customers, but I notice we only talk about the prostitutes and never the customers.

On my way home, I saw a few of our girls on the corner of the road. They spotted me, but wouldn't make eye contact while they were 'on duty'. I wanted to take them away and give them a hot drink, some food and a chance to sit beside a hot fire – BUT I couldn't. I know they hate what they do – so much so that the other day one of these girls gave her children to Social Services. She says she has to work and she can't do mother as well. She is too young for these choices. She is only a child herself. All around the area people complain about the girls and I think "there but for the grace of God go I". WHY, why do they have to do this work? And they wouldn't do it if they didn't have the customers. I don't understand.

I keep thinking of the woman at the well and her silent trip to a well at the hottest part of the day. I think of the way that some people seem to live their lives always in public view and open to public criticism. And then I think of these girls and how easy it is to drive by and judge. It is so public for them, but if I want an honest response to a direct question, then one of these girls will give it to me. They don't hide the reality of their lives – they may hide the reasons, but not the acts. I am thinking of so many different ways of being a prostitute without standing on a street corner. It is so easy to stay in a situation because of the financial gain; or to insist on doing a favour in order to gain advantage; or cover up to help a friend.

All the little (and large) events where I can prostitute myself and compromise my values so I don't lose face or station. And I know that these girls would be clued in enough to remind me of all of this should I have the courage to ask.[2]

Natalie is one of these girls, living and working on the streets for years. Even though she is still quite young, the toll her 'trade' has taken on her is severe. I know Natalie from her visits to the day centre. She is a lively soul, who can break and mend hearts in a matter of moments. Whenever she comes in, her presence is felt in the entire building. She can irritate and frustrate the most dedicated of workers, but comes up trumps at Christmas with gifts and seasons greetings for all.

I watch her closely and am intrigued by her behaviour. I see her arrive and watch her hold court with her peers. Natalie has very sad eyes and when she looks at you, you can see a sad and broken life ooze out. She doesn't cry with tears, but she cries from her core. She stands before you and makes a deep, hollow cry that emanates from her gut. She looks longingly and I don't know how to respond. All I can do is serve her dinner and hope it will suffice.

I imagine that some day I will have the courage to sit down with her and have a proper conversation, but most days she is high on either alcohol or drugs, or both. She is not easy to approach and then again, she has no problem approaching me with a gift and a huge "thank you for all you do for me". I rarely know where to turn, so I smile and say, "You're welcome. See you soon again".

Natalie obviously finds our day centre a safe place and has on occasion been pursued into the centre by the police following after one of her shoplifting sprees. There is no cure for her, just allow her come, eat and be Natalie. She regularly disappears for

2 Personal Journal, 30 June 1999

periods of a few months and we find out later that she has spent a term 'inside'. Prostitutes are often jailed and no sooner are they released than they are back at work. It's a revolving door which never stops turning, but that is her life and she can't change it for the moment.

I don't have the experience to help me reach out to Natalie in what I consider to be a constructive way. I can see such potential in her and I watch the way she comes and goes, but reaching out requires huge backup with teams of medical staff, counsellors and social workers. The obstacles in her way include her addictions to alcohol and drugs. Added to these is her prostitution, and of course, the illnesses associated with prostitution. These alone appear to be insurmountable, but then there is the low self-esteem, unworthiness, anger and much more. I don't have the words for all the other feelings she experiences and I don't believe Natalie could sit down and name them either. Her life is filled with addiction, prostitution and illness.

She comes in one day before Christmas with her arms full of gifts. She gift-wraps packets of biscuits for different friends who also frequent the day centre. She presents the centre director with a potted plant while others get hugs and kisses. I smile and wonder where she got all the gifts. I can't help wondering if the police will be calling on foot of a shoplifting claim. On this occasion there was no such claim and her plant is now blooming in the garden.

I often think of Natalie and enquire after her when she is missing for extended periods. When she is missing for a while and is known not to be in jail, we check the hospitals. One of the major fears for all involved in prostitution is AIDS and in time, I hear that Natalie has been diagnosed with AIDS. She is a danger to herself and her clients and if she does not take care of herself she will die. Unlike others I journey with, she is not put off by the threat of a death sentence. Her addictive personality convinces her of her indestructibility on the one hand, and conflicts with her desire to die and leave all this mess behind her, on the other. It is like a weighing scales tilting this way and then the other a few times each day.

I am torn inside watching her sharing gifts and watching her killing herself. She doesn't fully understand the path she is on. The highs she gets from alcohol and drugs blinds her to the reality of her situation. The support of the other street people boosts her in her resolve to continue in her street business. Her addictions numb and protect her from the reality all around her. No matter how difficult it is for her to fully comprehend the depth of her situation, I believe the truth trickles into her psyche over time. I believe she sees her life slip away from her on a roller coaster of self-destruction. Her prostitution is necessary to pay for the fixes, and the fixes drag her lower and lower, leaving her totally dependent on others to provide for the basics. She comes to us for food, to others for shelter and to the hospital for medical attention. It is like a huge scaffolding project around a crumbling building.

Natalie crumbles before our eyes as her health deteriorates and her dependency increases. As she crumbles, the cry from her gut groans louder. She is hard to deal with and grows more unpredictable. She is often left to look after herself and is encouraged to take her seat with the other diners. The noise is grating on everyone's nerves and before long there are potential fights stirring up all over the dining room. She is not happy at all, and it is not clear what is to be done, if anything can be done.

Natalie disappears again and no one is too upset. The dining room is calmer for her absence and it is easier for everyone to get on. I notice her absence, but I have no idea where she is. I walk home one morning and I think a lot about Natalie. I am used to the route I walk and before I know it, I am daydreaming. The daydream really shakes me to the core and leaves me quite anxious and numb. The dream is short and precise.

I am standing in front of Natalie and I can see nobody else. There is a grey background all around her, like partitions. She is waving her arms as if holding a weapon that I can't see. I call out to her: "Natalie, give me that, give it to me now, please." She continues waving her arms, and I hear the sound of others telling me to get back, that she'll kill me. I call to her again, ignoring the voices and I ask her again to give me the thing she is holding. "Natalie, give it to me, please, give it to me now." I am pleading while the voices behind me continue to warn me off. Her waving arms are still threatening me and a third time I call her by name and ask her to give me what she is holding. Suddenly, there is silence. I notice blood everywhere and I wipe the blood splatter from my clothes. I am not sure if she has killed me. NO, she has killed herself. Her weapon was a syringe.[3]

I do my best to erase the dream from my memory, but it rocks me. It is all so real, so real I can feel Natalie's presence with me for the next few hours. I go to the day centre, still shaken but looking out for Natalie. Part of me is convinced she will walk in and have her dinner. She doesn't come. Other clients who do come, arrive with the story that Natalie is dead. I have to know how, when and where she died. I don't talk about the dream until I get a chance to speak to the director in private. It takes time for him to check the hospitals for me and he comes back with the confirmation of her death. She died earlier in the morning, alone in a hospital bathroom, 'shooting up'. I know she wasn't alone and even though Natalie and I never really talked, we connected in a very different and real way.

---

3 Personal Journal, 2 June 2001

Two years later I happen to be in the same general hospital, and find the exact same colour grey walls as were in the dream. I think of her often and think of all the lives she saved by 'shooting up' that day. Had she gone back out on the streets to work, many more would now be very sick people. I don't know if there was a clearly thought-out motive behind her death, or if it was an accident. I learned the hard way that day that I couldn't fix Natalie, and maybe Natalie did not want to be fixed.

When I think of her, I recall the many sides to her life and personality. As always, I look to nature for some comfort and think of a rose. Some years before I ever met Natalie, I wrote a reflection in my journal about a red rose. It was a dark time for me, but there is a confidence in me that the darkness is not forever. Watching Natalie locked in her world, disintegrating before our eyes, I am reminded of this dark period of my life when I too was locked in circumstances beyond my control and disintegrating, until the time was right to move beyond the problems to bloom again.

A rose growing, a bud bursting to bloom, the centre exposed – what do I see? I see the dirt, the soil, dark and unwanted, something to be washed away, waste. I see friends in birds, fish, mountains, streams and rivers. Enemies are all around but reluctant to approach, to touch, to be soiled. But I see in the soil the richness of the depths which gives life to flowers, trees, food, animals, fish and provides essentials for shelter and life for a lot of what is not visible to the human eye. Soil gives life to this rose, which protects itself with hidden thorns. I see a deep red rose hidden in the green protective cover, burst to new life, rich in colour and smell. The heart of the flower is the engine for new birth and more growth. There I can hide, reflected in the centre, hidden in the beauty of the rose and protected by the thorns, confident that the seasons will hold me safe for extended periods. I marvel at the sun, mountains, streams, river, birds, fish and my beautiful rose with my reflection in it, aiming for the sun, but grounded deep in the earth, being fed and nurtured by the dirty soil. But I'm not in the rose, only my reflection is. I am buried in the dirt and feeding other life. I watch with envy the rest of creation grow and appear to thrive. My day will come – I know it will. In the meantime I'll keep giving life through me.[4]

Can I say I am so different from Natalie? There are times when I know I have sold myself short and entered into the soil. I also long to be beautiful like the rose but I am reluctant to be that visible. I am beginning to accept that all of us are nourishing each other in the soil and in the rose.

4 Personal Journal, 12 October 1998

BRIAN

God has created me to do Him some definite service[1]

Brian is setting off for Australia today to take up his new appointment as a parish priest there. His studies in Ireland are completed in record time and he is off to pastures new in his homeland. He is not very good at goodbyes, so we simply say "See you" at the airport. He walks away to the departure gates and then comes back and gives me a big hug. I fight back the tears as I agree to visit him in Australia. He has already written to his friends about those who looked after him while he was a student in Ireland and they are preparing to host us and check to see if we are as "unusual" as he has written.

It is summer when he leaves and a visit down-under would have to be at least a year away. Brian and I stay in touch as best we can. I phone him the day before Christmas Eve to let him know that my father is about to die. His curate takes the message and Brian phones back just as he is about to say the first Mass of his Christmas celebration. He doesn't know what to say, except that he is sorry and that he'll say the Mass for my father. For me there is nothing else he can do.

---

1 Newman, Cardinal John Henry. Meditations on Christian Doctrine; Hope in God, 6 March 1848

I phoned so many people today to let them know that Dad's death is imminent. I was hoping to talk to Brian but he is out on duty. The time difference and the echo on the line make the conversation sound weird. His poor curate was full of the joys of the festive season when I gave him the message for Brian. I didn't dress it up at all – I simply said "tell Brian that I phoned and that my father had a heart attack on Monday and today [Wednesday], the doctors advised us that the machines would be turned off. Please let him know that the machines are off now and we expect the sad news soon." I feel so cruel this evening having left the message so coldly for Brian. I don't know what else I can do. Why wasn't he in? I wanted so much for him to say something to help lift this dreadful burden I feel.[2]

A few days later, a card arrives in the post with all the lovely words he himself cannot say or write. He writes at the bottom – "I don't have the words but the card says what's in my heart". This is the first time we have encountered sadness in our friendship. All other incidents seem minor by comparison.

Just over a year after Brian returns to Australia, I make my trip south. I am quiet and still grieving my own loss of recent months and Brian is not used to seeing me like this. I am usually the joker in the pack. We don't talk about how it is for me. We do talk, but about everything other than the death. That is the way he operates and at this time of my life it suits me. I am too upset to engage with Brian in a heart to heart about someone as dear to me as my own father. The risk of opening up so far from home makes me feel vulnerable and isolated. I would risk it with him if I were at home and could go for long walks in familiar places. Nothing is familiar in Australia. It is a new world and very different to the one from which I have temporarily escaped.

---

2 Personal Journal, 23 December 1992

I love the people in Australia. They have such a different outlook on life and appear to be less caught up in material things. I am witnessing a wonderful respect for nature and all kinds of life. Away from the pressures of the city and the intensity of our combined family grief, I am beginning to see a new way forward. We don't talk about all that has happened, but I feel comforted and cared for. It feels good here and I can see how well Brian fits in with his 'flock'.[3]

Time flies when one is busy and it is soon four years since I left Brian to the airport that first time. He returns to Ireland on a visit with some of his Australian classmates – three lads on their summer holidays! They use my home as base and we have a terrific few days travelling around the country. They can only stay a few days since Ireland is just a stopover on a much bigger trip. It is hard to know how to make the most of the time without overdoing it.

There is a small party on one evening and the next day is dedicated to a day trip out of town. Being a small country, it is easy to get into the heart of the country within an hour of home, so we set off for lunch in the midlands followed by a drive in the countryside. I discover that one of Brian's friends, Frank, trained in Ireland just over forty years before and I set off to find his former college. It has changed hands over the years and I do manage to find the place with some help from the locals.

As we drive up the entrance to this large house, Frank starts to remember his time there and how times and places have changed since then. There is no one around, so we get out of the car and take a walk in the grounds. At the back of the building, in the distance, there are two columns of large maple trees. Frank suddenly stops and looks along the lines of trees. As he does, he says, "I helped

---

3 Personal Journal, 28 July 1993

plant those trees – over forty years ago". We stop in our tracks to look and admire his work. As I look, I think of all he might have done in the intervening years, and these trees have stayed put, rooted in the earth, reaching for the sky.

Even though Brian and I don't get many chances to meet, these trees are a reminder that even though I may stay put, I am growing and when we meet up, the growth is visible and real. The same is for Brian and how he has grown in his homeland with friends like Frank alongside. Nothing ever stays the same even though I often think otherwise.[4]

Frank strolls through the grounds and tells us about a walled garden that he used to work in. We turn a corner and there he finds the walled garden. It isn't as well tended these days, but the main features of the garden are still visible. For Frank, this is a real trip down memory lane and he starts telling stories about life in this college. "How come you ended up here, so far from home?" I ask. "Well," he says, "I was in my first year in college studying law and my cousin was going to Ireland to study for the priesthood. I went down to the quayside to wave him off and six months later I found myself on a similar liner heading to Ireland for study for the priesthood as well. It was 1953." A part of me gets such a surprise at how the course of a person's life can be changed so much by an event as simple as seeing a cousin off at the quayside.

Times were very different back then and residential students weren't allowed out without special permission, but of course Frank used to find ways around this. A particular family in a nearby village was very good for taking him to their home for the holiday breaks and some weekend treats. He remembers the name of the town they were from and we set off to find their

4 Personal Journal, 21 September 1995

home. We think it will be an education for Brian since after all, Frank had spent more time in Ireland than Brian and he was now enjoying regaling us with his tales.

Very little has changed in the village since he had been a young student. As we drive up a very narrow road, he shouts at me to stop. He recognises a house. We have arrived at his friends' home. Given that forty years have passed since he was a student, it is hardly likely that the family is still around. He had told us that the family had a lovely young daughter and I can see he is reminiscing about her and probably wondering what she is up to now. With that, a woman appears at the door – it's the 'lovely young daughter', now a fully-grown woman. She recognises Frank as he walks up and there is a big welcome.

We are all invited in to meet her father, the old man of the house who is now well advanced in years and quite feeble. When we walk in, he looks at Frank and smiles. "Well Frankie, I was only thinking of you the other day. How are you?" Frank is barely able to hold back the tears. It is as if the years melt away in the greeting. There is talk over a cup of tea and then we leave. We don't delay at all. The three of us find the day a little too nostalgic and emotional. I am delighted we made the trip, but I am also delighted to be on my way home.

I loved Frank's face when we walked into that house today. The old man was so pleased to see him after all the years. The years simply disappear when old friends get together again. I felt like Cilla Black in the TV show Surprise Surprise. I would hate however to be launched into my past like Frank was today – I hope he enjoyed it once he got over the initial shock. It was so special being in the place he had studied and worked in all those years ago, plus the added bonus of meeting his friends. It was an eye opener for Brian too – a little insight into a time they would not have known each other. I am so grateful for days like this and I am grateful for the chance to act on impulse and just go – carpe diem![5]

Brian's visit is so short, but it is much better than the letters or the very brief phone calls. While I love the letters, there is nothing to beat human, face-to-face interaction. As my own circumstances change, I am unable to travel, but Brian is in contact during this period and he decides to travel to Ireland again on a stopover during a pilgrimage to the Holy Land. The pilgrimage is organised by one of the Catholic groups near his parish and he is invited to go as their spiritual director. Rather than return to Australia and then set off on his annual leave, he decides to extend the pilgrimage trip, and visit a few of us over here.

The long gaps between our visits often highlight how we change as we get older. Things seem not to change and then someone like Brian pays a visit and suddenly our 'newness' is evident, reflected through the eyes of the visitor. I notice Brian has changed too and he is becoming more open to talking and expressing his own feelings. My home is once more his base for part of this short stopover and, once again, we travel each day to different places, catching up on everyone. It is great fun but as always it goes too fast.

We enjoy lots of lovely meals, theatre outings, drinks out and great walks in the unpredictable Irish July weather. We all marvel at how well he looks. While he is visiting, he discovers that one of his younger fellow students has succumbed to a serious illness. He is lucky that not only is he feeling well, the hearing problems that were once a source of great concern are not restricting him at all. As we say goodbye at the airport, we promise to meet up again as soon as we can. The distance and cost are prohibitive for

5 Personal Journal, 21 September 1995

me at the moment, but it's nice dreaming. In the meantime, we re-engage in letters and phone calls.

A few weeks pass and I check my phone messages to hear "Hi, it's Brian here. I've got cancer". I ring back as soon as I can. Brian explains that he had some tests and cancer was found in his oesophagus. It is operable, he tells me, and he is going to meet with all sorts of medics for advice, support and surgical intervention. Surgery is planned, along with chemotherapy and radiotherapy. He will be off work for five months and then return to work on a phased basis. He rattles off all the medical stuff and it is hard for me to understand it in one short call. He is so matter of fact about the procedures and the prognosis.

The phone call from Brian shocked me. I sobbed when I put the phone down and now as I write I'm wondering WHY. Why Brian? This illness is getting a strong grip on too many of our friends. He looked so well a few weeks ago. I am hoping the tests are wrong. This is very hard to deal with at this distance. I want to see him and hear him tell me the same information face to face. Not possible – for now. Another waiting game starts and fingers crossed that the path he is choosing will work out. Thy will, not mine be done, but please make him well again.[6]

Brian is not very good at talking about his feelings, even though there has been some improvement in this area. Every time I try to talk at a level beyond the facts, he cuts me off. It is so difficult to have a serious conversation with him on the phone, but it's all we have for the foreseeable future. The news is heartbreaking for me and now I have to let the rest of our friends know what is happening to him all those thousands of miles away. I tell them exactly what Brian has told me and I try to be as emotionless as I

6 Personal Journal, 8 August 1999

can. Of course, the tears flow as soon as I put the phone down to each of them, or as soon as I transmit the email message.

I am in constant communication with Australia and am delighted to hear that the surgery goes very well and, instead of Brian being out of action for five months, he is up and active in two months. The doctors are very pleased with his progress and he is keen to do everything they tell him to do in order to beat his illness. He reads all the literature he can find and follows the professionals' advice. Probably, for the first time since childhood, he is accepting help from friends, colleagues and neighbours.

I find him better able to talk about how he is feeling rather than talking about the awful facts of his illness. Something has changed in Brian and it is wonderful. His dice with death has possibly helped him to look differently at life. He has had so much time during the treatment to be himself and to look after himself, instead of always doing for others.

Brian is a very private man, but he is now having to get used to complete strangers doing intimate medical examinations. He now lies back and lets it happen. He is focusing on a full recovery. He meets with patients who have had similar surgery and he gets great support from them. He is also supporting patients embarking on the same course of treatment that he has come through. He is starting to move into his feelings and our conversations are developing and growing at a new level. The phone is still very hard, but as he gets better, he is more positive, more spiritual and more aware of things he has never mentioned before.

The news we all hope for comes at Easter, just a few months after the treatment ends. Brian is given the all-clear and his brief tangle with death has passed him by. The grim reaper is not ready to check him in to a new 'resting place'. He is starting to question why he has been cured and wonders about the task which he must complete before he will be allowed to die. However, he is still so pleased and grateful for this second chance that he decides to make a trip to the Holy Land in thanksgiving. He is very familiar with the Holy Land and has spent a number of holidays and pilgrimages pursuing his personal, scriptural and spiritual journey through the places he knows so well from his studies and his ministry.

Brian and I have often had wonderful conversations about the foundations of our Christian church and our own Christian beliefs. It may sounds terribly serious but we find a human and even comical side to it all. I tease him about the power and strength of the women in Scripture, contrasting these traits with the denials and betrayals of some of the men. Once the bait is set, we both debate the issues, neither of us giving in to the other and both of us using all our resources to put forward our argument. Brian always wins due to his extensive studies in church matters and over twenty-five years in active ministry. Yes, I'm the mouse taking on the heavyweight champion in his own field.

I am so pleased hearing about the all-clear from Brian and I look forward to seeing him soon again. It feels like years since we last met, even though it is only a year. It's like waking up from a dreadful nightmare. All going well, he will have a longer stopover in Ireland when he makes his pilgrimage. It is a miracle, the kind normally witnessed only in movies. He is delighted that his patience and rigorous attention to the medication, exercise and advice have paid off. He is also very aware of the divine hand in all of this, and is in close contact with his mortality. He reminds me of Lazarus, brought back from the other side. Being so far from Brian during the illness, I believe he withheld a lot of the pain and suffering he went through. He always managed to be upbeat, even when delivering bad news. Now he sees he has a new chance at life and it's up to him to live it to the full.

He got the all-clear – I can't believe it! I want to give him a big hug and welcome him back to life. During the last months, I was anticipating his death everyday and preparing myself for the phone call telling me he had died. Well, no longer do I have to live in fear of this. He is coming back to celebrate with the Irish gang after he has said 'thanks' in the Holy Land. I am so looking forward to being with him after the appalling year he has put in – I bet he sees things differently now. I hope he sees things differently now. What joy letting everyone here know the good news – good news at long last.[7]

The plans for the return visit are well under way and I am planning all sorts of surprises for Brian. Fortunately, I am able to take time off so that we can travel wherever and whenever he wants. I am delighted about the visit, but also apprehensive. It is as if it is too good to be true. My apprehension is well founded and within weeks of getting the all-clear, the doctor tells him he has found more cancer.

It is just a few weeks before the trip and Brian already has the air tickets and hotel reservations. It is agreed that he will have four weeks of intensive radiotherapy, followed by one week of rest, and then he will fly to the Holy Land. His two friends will accompany him on his pilgrimage, and the Irish gang will look after him on this side. He is adamant that he will make this trip but he is concerned about travel insurance and his need to tell the airlines that he is so ill. He makes up a special first aid box with all his medication including emergency supplies. During this latest treatment, he adopts a routine of resting and meditation to keep him from over-tiring and he will continue to rest and meditate while on holidays.

I set off for the airport but the flight is delayed. It is already 10.30pm and I know he will be very tired when he does finally

---

7 Personal Journal, 21 March 2000

arrive. I hate all the waiting and worrying and wondering. I wonder how he is coping with the travelling, worry that I won't cope when I see him and worry that the effort of all the travelling will shorten his already very fragile life. I watch all the other people in the arrivals hall and imagine their stories, thinking of the sadness around my reasons for being there.

Brian comes out eventually and although tired, he is looking very well, a lot better than I expected. We briefly catch up on some news and I outline the plans I have for the few days we have together. He is open to the plans, but we agree that it is flexible and open to change if needs be.

I am surprised that I am not walking on eggshells as I had anticipated. Brian is open to talking about his illness, the all-clear and then the reverse of the all-clear – I can't believe it. I was anxious that he would be quite dependent, but he is happy to be left to rest and meditate while I am free to do other things. I thought I would feel tied, but his openness has loosened the ties I had feared. He is different – easier to be with and more honest about his life and impending death. This is hard for me – I never thought it would be like this with Brian even though my head knows about the cancer. This heart of mine always wants a fairytale ending, but I had this fairytale ending for just a few months and that was lovely – now I am back in reality and I know I have to stay strong for him. This is a heartbreaking journey for both of us as we set out to meet our friends for the last time.[8]

Our first trip is back to the West and lunch with a friend, Vincent. Vincent is off to the United States the next day and our conversation centres on this for a while. The two men then exchange stories about coping with chemotherapy and radiotherapy. For Vincent, the news is much better than for Brian, but there is not a hint

8 Personal Journal, 23 July 2000

of moaning from Brian. Quite the opposite, he is very grateful for the extra year and all the blessings it has brought. He doesn't begrudge Vincent his all-clear status and simply wishes him all the best. Both men are Newman scholars and Scripture scholars, and they acknowledge that all our lives have a distinct purpose on earth. Listening to them talking, I am reminded of the Cardinal Newman reflection.

God has created me to do Him some definite service; He committed some work to me which He has not committed to another. I have my mission – I may never know it in this life, but I shall be told it in the next. I am a link in a chain, a bond of connection between persons. He has not created me for naught. I shall do good; I shall do His work. I shall be an angel of peace, a preacher of truth in my own place while not intending it – if I do but keep His commandments.[9]

I excuse myself from lunch to buy food supplies for our next stop. I also need to take some time for myself. The two men continue their conversation before Brian and I set off by car for the neighbouring city and more people to meet. I love the meetings but I hate the farewells. I am wondering if it would not have been easier for the two of us to simply do tourist things and not engage so much with the past. I know Brian wants to engage with the past and he needs to say the goodbyes. I just find it so difficult.

It is wonderful to be with Brian, but am I being fair to him? I hope he is able for all the get-togethers that are lined up for the next few days. I guess he is free enough to tell me if he is finding it a problem. I feel so guilty that I cannot share fully in his pain. When he talks about the treatments, I know I can only listen. I have no idea about the real upset he has already endured, and cannot fully empathise.

---

9 Newman, Cardinal John Henry. Meditations on Christian Doctrine; Hope in God, 6 March 1848

Listening to him talking with Vincent, I am so pleased that there he has true listening and empathy. Yes, this journey is a good idea for all of us – even though it's hard watching him suffering; watching me suffering.[10]

As we say farewell to Vincent and his family, the effort of the afternoon is beginning to show on Brian. He uses the car journey to our next stop to catch up on rest and sleep. For the first time, I am fully aware of the cancer, and I really take on board the seriousness of his condition and its advanced stage. I start to note the towns which have good hospital facilities should I need to get emergency help for him. I grow nervous as we drive further west.

When we arrive at our next stop, we let ourselves into the house and make up our rooms and put the supplies away. Our host meets us as we make our short journey into the town for our evening meal. I get used to the meetings and with each one I relax more and start to enjoy them. I get used to hearing Brian tell his story and as I hear it again and again, it grows on me. It becomes part of me and part of this holiday. There is no dwelling on the illness, but there is space for Brian to enjoy the break in an environment that honours him as a human being and honours his current circumstances. I find that our friends create what I call a sacred space, something that is impossible to describe but recognisable when presented.

Brian has retired early and I enjoy being able to relax in front of the fire. It has been an emotional day for me watching him with all the different people. A lot is said, and a lot more is left unsaid. As we leave each person, there was no sense of unfinished business – it feels right from my perspective and Brian seems peaceful. I still feel anxious for him and for me. I am anxious that someone will

10 Personal Journal, 24 July 2000

say something to upset him and I feel the onus is on me to be his protector. I am grateful that his friends are also my friends and they are very supportive of me as I make this trip.[11]

Brian and I get a chance to recharge our batteries and Brian feels free enough to rest and meditate. He is great for falling in with lunch dates and brief encounters and I marvel at the apparent ease with which he meets people and enjoys their company. I notice though how the encounters tire him a little more each day. He insists, however, on being fully part of the holiday and going to as many places as possible. The extent of his illness is apparent again on our trip into the city. After a short walk through a few shops, we have to sit and rest three times before we eventually make it home in time for him to take a well-earned sleep.

I want to run away and cry. He is not able for even a short walk these days and he isn't able to hide his frailty anymore. It is hard to be the minder for someone who is normally so strong. I was so pleased to bury myself in housework while he slept in preparation for our dinner out this evening.[12]

Our dinner guests come to visit us at my home and we have dinner in a nearby hotel. We leave the hotel quite early and walk home where our guests say their farewells on the doorstep. They feel Brian needs a rest and so the evening ends very early. It is difficult for them to leave, but Brian and I wave them off.

Brian looks at me and suggests going back out to the same hotel for an Irish whiskey. We go straight back and enjoy a relaxing drink and relaxing conversation with traditional music in the background. The waitress gets a surprise when she sees the two of us back so

---

11 Personal Journal, 24 July 2000
12 Personal Journal, 26 July 2000

soon. "I thought you left earlier," she says with a quizzical look on her face. "Yeah, we did," I answer, "we had to let our 'serious friends' go home early. Now we're back for the 'serious fun'."

It is great that he is able to come out with me again. I need to take a break from the intensity of some of our conversations – conversations about his prognosis and conversations about state and church matters. The holiday pace slows down and we decide to take the pressure off the two of us by availing of a tourist bus trip of the city. It is ideal as we sit on top listening to a hilarious commentary and enjoying our fellow tourists. We finally alight close to a coffee shop where we enjoy a wonderful cappuccino. Brian laughs that he doesn't have to watch his diet anymore and that he can fully enjoy all the things he had been told were unhealthy. The day is rounded off with the arrival of another guest, Brendan. It is great the way so many of our friends have been available to meet us. I have a real sense that it is meant to be.

When the last day of Brian's break with me arrives, I am relieved that our time together has gone well for both of us. We manage to contact one more person, a great friend now living in Boston. We enjoy a four-way conversation by phone before Brian, Brendan and I adjourn to have lunch with my family. I can feel the strain as they say goodbye to him. Everyone leaves us and once more it is just Brian and me.

My final task is to drop him out to a nearby town so he can have a few days with yet another friend, Mary. He delays as long as possible and then asks me do a detour along the scenic route before reaching her home. The three of us enjoy a lovely meal where we talk very openly about the future. She later tells me that she is quite nervous about his visit and I am so relieved. I thought I was the only one to experience this kind of anxiety. It is great having someone to talk to who understands that this is not easy.

Handing Brian over to Mary was very hard – it was time for me to say goodbye and I didn't like it at all. I know we will meet again before he dies, but I know I have to waste no time in arranging my visit to him. He has put such effort into this trip, it's my turn now. There is no time for dithering.[13]

Brian and I are back to telephone calls and the long distance between us is more evident than ever. His visit was wonderful and I decide to travel to Australia to see him again. It is only a few weeks since he came over and now I am on a flight south with my sister. The trip is long and I am apprehensive about how he will be when we meet this time, and how I will deal with what I find. Brian had complained while he was with me about a pain in his knee and he has been told that it is arthritis. He tells me, though, that he believes it is the cancer spreading.

With this kind of talk from him, I know that he must be in a very bad way. If he is now recognising the spread of cancer then I believe the extent of his illness is worse again – I pray I am wrong.[14]

Our first few days in Australia are spent resting and getting over the jetlag. We get a chance to meet Brian's friends and I am surprised at his unwillingness to talk about the reality of his illness with them. This is very different from my experience of being with him when meeting our friends in Ireland. When the state of his illness is brought up in conversation, the subject is changed or he is told that he is looking great. He knows he isn't great and I sense some upset on his part that his reality is denied him.

Brian takes my sister Eileen and me away on a trip to the desert. The further we go out of the city, away from the noise and all the people, the more I find myself relaxing into the vastness and beauty

13 Personal Journal, 28 July 2000

14 Personal Journal, 18 August 2000

of this place. Our journey takes us north along lovely fast toll roads and before long we are on smaller roads surrounded by green fields and farmlands. Every now and then, we pass a huge crop of wheat and the whole scene changes colour. As the wind blows, the wheat waves us on to our next town. Further on there is a field of yellow, perhaps sunflowers, swaying and nodding at us. We are surrounded by colour and life and, in a strange way, I sense it acknowledge our presence in a gentle and affirming manner.

There is a point on our journey when we have to stop for a break and to refuel the car and ourselves. Beyond this point, there is little in the way of supplies or creature comforts. There are a few outposts where the mines used to be and we are going to stay in one of these. I am excited and curious as we resume the journey to the desert. Driving along, I am struck by the narrow line of electric pylons and the overhead cables. Between the cables and the ground, a heat shimmer is clearly visible. The extent of the heat is disguised by the air conditioning in the car itself, but the lack of life, human, animal or plant, indicates that it is an unbearable heat.

We drive beyond the last town at the edge of the desert into a place with no other human beings in sight. We stop and I get out of the car to take a closer look. What looked like a barren uninhabitable land is populated with the most wonderful flowers and shrubs. These plants survive in conditions the majority of humans would not contemplate. None of this life was visible as we drove up. To the naked eye, the terrain looks dead and empty. But there is life in this place and it is absolutely wonderful once we step out of the car and become part of it. Brian looks to the vastness beyond and reminds me that he will be part of it soon, as soon as his task on earth is complete. This kind of talk is so like the way Mark used to talk. Brian is in touch with nature and creation. It is as if he is being drawn back to his source as Mark was only a few years ago. History is repeating itself, but this time I appear to be in Laurie's shoes. Now I am beginning to understand the wider picture around the journey with Mark.

I love the desert and all it represents. I see in it the vast eternity and my own finiteness. It has everything it needs to survive although it appears to have nothing – appearing worthless in its entire expanse. But isn't that its joke on us – it is priceless beyond our human limitation. Scripture tells us that not a single grain of sand exists but that God knows about it. As the three of us stand looking out, I am comforted as I remember this, and know in my heart that all my pain, suffering and joys actually do have a reason. Knowing the reason is the challenge. I am so lucky to be here to see this and know this. The sun disappears quickly and before I know it I can no longer see the desert. The moon is bright, but all I can see appears changed. It is not the same desert anymore, and yet it is. It just looks different in this light. And that's the way with Brian. He is different in the light of his illness, yet he is the same. I am different in the light of his illness, yet I am the same. I want to stay here in the desert and simply listen to it teach me all the things about life and death that I have been worrying about before flying out here. I feel the calmness of this place, but I know that there are times it is involved in the most violent of storms that uproot the tiny flowers and cacti. It is just like my own life with all its ups and downs. Nature is my best teacher if I but take the time to sit and listen.[15]

From the desert we journey south to the ocean. The contrast is striking and once again I find that nature gives both Brian and me freedom to speak from our hearts. As we look out on the ocean beating relentlessly on the shore, we question the return of his illness and the reasons for the reprieve for a short while.

15 Personal Journal, 7 September 2000

"Why," he asks, "did I get an extra year?" "I guess, to do what you are doing," I respond. I believe in my heart that this physical journey is also a huge part of his spiritual journey and also of my spiritual journey now. The more we engage in the heart and soul of ourselves, the more in touch we become with our own inner selves and our purpose for being.

We continue watching the water lashing the stone of the cliffs and we acknowledge the water will continue lashing the coast long after either or both of us have died. Of course, this dying is not at a time to be decided by humans. After all, my plane might crash on the return flight and I might very well be waiting on the other side for Brian to arrive. The very idea brings a smile to his face. Imagine flying thousands of miles to see him before he dies and then being at the Pearly Gates ahead of him. He loves the irony and he loves the way I don't mind talking and laughing about our living and dying.

We seem to spend an eternity at the ocean, just looking out. At one viewing point there is a series of standing stones called the Twelve Apostles. With a glint in his eye, Brian asks me to name a few. I tell him that the two stones standing close together must be the brothers James and John, jostling for the prime position on the podium with Jesus. He knows from our many conversations that I wouldn't see eye to eye with Peter, so he asks me where Peter is. There is one standing stone which rises out of the water a few metres, with a second stone on top of it, a little to one side, and then a third stone on the top in line with the first. "This is my Peter," I tell him "because he can't decide which way is up for him. He's not quite sure of the direct way to God. He goes up a bit, then moves off on a tangent and then comes back in line." It is also me. This is my personal journey to God too. It is also Brian's journey and maybe it is everyone's journey to their God.

I love talking with Brian about the Scriptures and our place in them and he tells me he enjoys the simple way I own the stories and the characters therein. I don't ever think of them as being simple, I think of them as being as real to me today as they were two thousand years ago. And just as the waters are beating against this coast that we are standing at today, they beat against it hundreds of years ago and they will be beating against it in hundreds of years to come for a new set of people to marvel at. This is life and this is our mortality within it. Just as the maple trees outlived Frank's term as a student, so they will outlive his life on earth. If those maple trees could talk, they would speak of thousands of families from every continent without ever having moved beyond the spot in which they were first planted.

As with the desert, I find it hard to move back to the car and back to where we are staying for the night. I want so much to stay put because here I feel real and in touch with my soul and inner being. Here, in this wonderful natural phenomenon, I feel free enough to speak from my heart and soul. Brian is drawing me out as much as I am drawing him out. There is peace, and if dying means returning to the earth and joining all of this nature, then I feel a great peace around my own mortality – dare I say I even look forward to my eternity in the middle of God's wonderful patchwork quilt, which is nature.[16]

Back in the 'real' world, we are confronted by the fact that when we look well, people only see the image and won't accept the reality behind the image. Time and time again, Brian grows tired and upset by the denial of others of his illness. I find it hard to agree with him when he tells me he is dying, but I have to agree with him because it is the truth. Others are finding it hard to agree with him, because to do so brings home to them that, very soon,

---

16 Personal Journal, 8 September 2000

their dear friend will be gone from them forever. As we watch the opening ceremony of the Sydney Olympics with Brian and his friends, I am struck by the fact that because they love him so much, they are afraid to admit that he is not going to be around for his next birthday which is a little less than a year away.

"Next year we're going to have a party for your birthday," they say. "The two girls will come back and we'll have your family and other friends too." He looks at me, half smiles and then says to them, "Go ahead with the party, but I won't be here. I'll be gone". I nod discreetly at him confirming what he has said. His Australian friends get very upset with him but no one is quite sure what to say in reply.

The subject is changed and everyone returns to watching the Olympic flame being lit. As we share that great moment in history with millions of people throughout the world, I cannot distract myself from the talk of the birthday party. I will never watch the footage of those Olympics without remembering that night. Their hopes for his next birthday are a wonderful expression of their love, but it is hard for him hearing the denial of his truth behind their unquestioning love.

Today when we talked about dying, Brian questioned his fears – "why should anyone be afraid of dying? When I was born, I came into the world with nothing. I arrived safely into the arms of the nursing staff who made sure I was healthy and then gave me to my mother who nursed me and cared for me. I came from the total darkness of the womb into the unknown that is this world. Soon I will leave this world with absolutely nothing and I will be received into the arms of Jesus. A new-born once more – in a new world." And he is right – why the fears? I know I can't survive the day without worrying umpteen times over ridiculous things – things I have no control over or input into and even things that have nothing to do with me. I just worry and then miss out on the living.[17]

All too soon this holiday is over and I know it is the last time I will see him alive. I do all I can to honour his situation by telling the truth and in doing so, I have to put aside some of my own feelings in order to appear brave for him. I won't allow myself to get upset in front of him.

As we embrace at the departure gates, he asks me to "come back if you can". I want to say yes, but I can't because I know in my heart that he won't be around long enough for me to be able to travel again. I walk through the departure gates in the airport, glancing back for a second just to have a last look. Eileen walks close by me but we say nothing. With the corner of my eye I can see him looking so sad as we go on our way. I say nothing because I know that if I utter one word, I will break down under the overwhelming sense of grief and sadness I feel. Even though I am holding back the tears, the very effort at holding so much consumes and drains me. I cannot look back again, because I know he is only yards away but forever out of reach. I cling by a thread to St Paul's promise that we are given no trial on earth that we cannot cope with.

Walking through the inner sanctum of this large international airport, I am upset and angry with God for taking another friend away. The dreadful thing is that Brian is not yet dead, but for me, about to fly thousands of miles to the other side of the world, he feels dead to me and a huge part of me is dying with him. In the final embrace, I hand Brian over to his family and friends while I exit from his world. I now have only the telephone and electronic mail, a new feature which I set up while I was at his home.

---

17 Personal Journal, 15 September 2000

It was so hard for me to say goodbye and hand him over to others to care for him. I think my chest will burst with the ache I feel in my heart. I now understand the term 'a broken heart' – my heart feels smashed as if it is about to explode out of my chest cavity. Even though I feel rotten and I am so angry with God for dealing out all this pain to so many people, I wouldn't swap our friendship for all the treasures in the world. I am so appreciative for having the chance to be with him, and having Eileen with us has been great for me in the midst of all of the upset. Returning to work and the normal working week tomorrow – I wish I were back at the ocean or in the middle of the desert.[18]

The weeks go by quickly and before long Christmas is upon us. In the meantime, the word from Australia is not good. The 'arthritis' is in fact cancer as Brian had suggested back in the summer. He is very angry about this diagnosis and very upset that the doctors hadn't listened to him from the outset. He still trusts his doctors, but he is not happy. He is not able to communicate too much so I use electronic mail to hear news from some of his Australian friends:

Our good friend Father Brian is not well. At present in hospital, cancer has spread. There is a tumour on the knee, outside of the bowel, and apparently he is full of it. Doctors have advised there is nothing they can do for him except control the pain. Sorry to be the bearer of tidings of such news, but thought you should know. With love … A[19]

When the news comes in, I send an email to our friends in Ireland to keep them up to date.

---

18 Personal Journal, 19 September 2000
19 Email from Australia, 17 November 2000

I phoned Brian last night and he was in better mood than I expected. He is annoyed that he suggested that there was a tumour on the knee months ago and they only found it now. They also found cancer cells in his ribs, breastbone and I think, shoulder. Internally, they found cells on the bowel. He says that he expected another all-clear, and is finding the amount of bad news a lot to handle. At this stage the doctors are planning treatments which will help the symptoms but he knows there is no cure. It is just a matter of allowing him to function as best he can in the circumstances for as long as he can. He has someone covering the parish for the next few weeks and then he hopes to be in a position to work again. A lot will depend on how weakening the treatment will be this time round. They are talking about radiotherapy to zap each of the bone cancers and chemotherapy to try and hit the bowel. It's a lot to ask at this stage and he is tired and worn out with all the tests and procedures.[20]

He returns to his work and manages to do the Christmas liturgies, but at a very high price. He grows very weak and I get the following update by electronic mail:

HAPPY NEW YEAR – Attended midnight Mass on Christmas Eve and had dinner with Fr Brian on the Friday evening (22nd December). Looked fair, could not believe it when I saw him Christmas Eve. Deteriorated so much. It is just so sad to see him. He walks with a walking stick, and has lost about 3 stone (or more) in weight. Now wears patches, to help with the pain. His colour is dreadful (almost think it had hit the liver). He tells me he has been in touch with you several times – that is good. Very hard to talk to him at present, in bed at 8.30 and I find it hard to find something to say. Love …A[21]

---

20 Email from author to friends in Ireland, 20 November 2000
21 Email from Australia, 1 January 2001

With every mail and every call, I feel there is a nipping away at this fragile life. The bad news goes on and on and I wish it was all over.

Really don't know if I should be telling you this, but unfortunately it is more sad and bad news. Father Brian had a fall on Tuesday evening and is in hospital. The news is not good. They performed an MRI and found thickening on the outer protection of the brain and also on the outer protection of the spine. Also his liver is not functioning properly. I saw him on Wednesday and I knew straight away there was something wrong with his liver. His colour was dreadful. Have talked to C tonight (Saturday 13th January) and she says that his attitude and faith are still very strong. I must be very greedy, I want God to take him home soon, yet at the same time I do not want to lose such a wonderful friend and human being. What does one do? Apparently his voice is now very weak, talking to him on the phone would now be very hard. It would be like talking from one end of a tunnel to another. Love … A[22]

I need to respond to this mail because I can relate so well with the sentiments enclosed. Despite the distance and the time difference, I find it possible to really engage with Brian's friends in cyberspace. I manage to reply:

I feel something like yourself when you say "I must be very greedy, I want God to take him home soon, yet at the same time I do not want to lose such a wonderful friend and human being. What does one do?" The rotten thing for me is that there is nothing I can do except pray that Brian is peaceful in himself and that all his friends and colleagues receive some of the same peace so that when he does die, it will be gentle for as many as possible. This has been a very difficult

22 Email from Australia, 13 January 2001

journey for all Brian's friends, but the manner in which he has lived through the last couple of years must have been a great inspiration to countless people. Thanks for keeping me up to date and I wish I could do something. My friends and myself continue praying for you all. The miracle I pray for now is peace and acceptance as the time moves on. Take care and much love … P[23]

Soon after this mail, the word comes to say that Brian is dead. I decide to have a special gathering in my home to celebrate his life and death with a Requiem Mass. It is decided to have this at a time as close as possible to the actual funeral Mass in Australia. In trying to get details of the events in Australia, I send the following note:

Can you tell me when the funeral is taking place? A few of us are going to try and gather around the same time in my home to join with you all in praying for Brian and for all his friends and family. Later in the month we are going to meet up in the West and celebrate him again – probably around the month's mind time. I can't believe how overwhelming I am finding the fact of Brian's death. I knew when I left in September that I could not fulfil his invitation to come back to see him. I knew getting on the plane that he would not live much longer than Christmas, but every part of me wanted me to be wrong, and hoped that he would last longer. The more I reflect on our friendship and the wonderful person he was, I know that the manner in which he died is going to be a source of great life for so many who witnessed his faith and the acceptance of the dreadful deterioration of his bodily functions and appearance. He certainly lived the final weeks as a real life Calvary before our very eyes, and over the telephone lines. Even as his body gave in, he still kept going. I have seen so many who give up at the first mention of illness, and lie down waiting to die. But Brian was a very special person. Since I

23 Email to Australia, 13 January 2001

came back from Australia, I have been enjoying the happy memories of the visit and of the previous ten years of our friendship. I am aware that you all start this journey of your own memories, but as long as we all remember and we all talk about Brian, he will never truly be dead. Brian has left us a lot to talk about and a lot to celebrate, but for the moment, I feel dreadfully sad and it all feels a bit too much to bear. We are very lucky to have met Brian and to have been allowed to know him. I also feel very lucky to have met so many of his Australian friends and I do hope that our friendship will continue. I wish with all my heart I could be with you at this time, but I cannot. I will, however, be connected with you in spirit. Love … P[24]

It is devastating for me and I ask myself "why is it devastating?" It is devastating because in the final few years, we lived with the truth and shared from our hearts, our souls and our minds. It is one of the most rewarding things I have ever done and probably one of the most painful.

For it was you who formed my inward parts; knit me together in my mother's womb. I praise you for the wonder of my being, for the wonder of all your works.[25]

As the journey on earth with Brian closes, I recognise the part Mark's journey played in preparing me for this. Newman's meditation is alive as I see the links between Mark and Brian and between Laurie and me. I believe, now more than ever, that every encounter has a purpose and each one is part of my growth. The journeys with Brian and Mark continue in a very different way now and we were right not to say goodbye, but to simply say "See you again", because every time I remember them, they are fully visible to me in my mind and alive in what I do.

---

24 Email to Australia, 18 January 2001
25 Psalm 139:13

PEGGY

I shall be an angel of peace[1]

It's Easter time. The homeless centre is now looking after an average of two hundred people each day and, at holiday times such as this, I am busy looking for volunteers to help out. As always, the helpers turn up and give fully of themselves. I am busy doing so many things, I am not really paying attention to the fact that it is Easter, nor am I living the Easter journey. I am going through the motions and not being fully present. I manage to get some quiet time in the middle of the noise, and I watch the faces of the people all around me. At the end of a busy day, I am pleased with myself for all that I have managed to do.

My contentment is shaken with news that Peggy is in hospital with a suspected broken hip. On the surface, it does not appear serious, but I am concerned because this is just the latest in a catalogue of health problems for Peggy, an elderly woman living alone in a house close to mine. She is retired, having worked all her life in the city centre. She is petite, meticulous about herself and her appearance, slow to ask for help and hates bothering doctors with what she believes are minor ailments. Peggy waits until she is obviously quite unwell before going for a diagnosis and medication.

---

1 Newman, Cardinal John Henry. *Meditations on Christian Doctrine; Hope in God,* 6 March 1848

She occupies herself with her friends and her part-time job which keeps her in touch with many of the local people.

Peggy's phone number came up on my caller ID and I now know that I missed a call for help from her while I was at the centre. Thankfully, she did get through to Clare who took her to hospital. Peggy rarely asks for help and when she does, I'm off somewhere else, unavailable to her. Maybe this hospital visit will put her back on the right track to full health – or will it be the end for her – I hope and pray NOT.[2]

Like all Christians, I associate Easter with death and resurrection. The sight of buds on the trees, new flowers in gardens and lots of colour in the countryside gives me great hope. It's springtime and there is a bursting forth of things new all around us. I phone Peggy in the hospital and she is in relatively good form. She spent some time in Accident & Emergency before being moved to a ward. A bank holiday is a hard time to be in hospital but Peggy is coping well. She needs surgery to repair the broken bone, but this is delayed due to the fact that she has fluid in her lungs. She sounds in good form and is grateful to be in a safe place where she is being cared for. I am delighted that she is now being looked after properly.

Peggy and I know each other for many years. This is, however, the first time that she has been so seriously ill and she is anxious about her job. She is worried about finding someone to fill in for her until she is fit enough to return to work. Despite reassuring her about the job, Peggy continues to worry. The more she worries, the more difficult it is for her to concentrate on getting well. Her surgery is postponed each day due to her breathing problem. Each morning she fasts until the late afternoon when the medical team unfortunately announce that, once more, the procedure has to be postponed. In effect, she spends most of the week fasting and, as

2 Personal Journal, 22 April 2000

a consequence, loses quite a lot of weight. Each time I visit her in hospital, she looks thinner than the day before.

The bright airy ward, filled with the colour of flowers and cards, is a sharp contrast to Peggy's frail situation and pale features. The pain at this stage is almost unbearable and it is visibly etched on her face. Even her eyeglasses appear to highlight how her face has shrunk in the few days. Thankfully, at the end of the week, her lungs are robust enough to cope with the surgery. I am concerned that while her lungs are stronger, her spirit is weaker and she appears to be more unwell than someone with a broken hip. I can't help but think the worst.

Peggy is now in hospital exactly one week. She has had the surgery and medically she is on the mend. Clare tells me, however, that she is very worried about her. She tells me that Peggy is very confused and speaking in a very strange way. She describes her as having a glazed look on her face and mumbling a lot. Clare's voice is so full of fear that I do not delay in calling up to the hospital. I find Peggy in a different ward staring into space, convinced that she is already dead. Her eyes look empty and far away. There is no energy in her at all. She is weak and lifeless. She cannot wear her glasses because the connections for her oxygen mask keep knocking them off. When she tries to put the glasses on her nose, she cannot breath properly so she has to visualise her surroundings based on the little that she can see combined with all the noises around her.[3]

This new ward is in an older part of the hospital and is much darker that the original ward Peggy was being looked after in. When I arrive the staff are busy with a very distressed patient and I notice that she grows upset with all the fuss and noise around this other woman. Not being able to see clearly contributes a lot

3 Personal Journal, 29 April 2000

to her upset. I gingerly walk down to her bed and sit beside her.

She recognises me after a short while and explains to me that she is in the "dying room". Trying not to look startled by the expression she has just used, I allow her to chat away in the hope that I can understand what is happening for her. The discussion moves disturbingly through different phases of her understanding of what is happening to her and all around her. "There is no point hanging around, I am dying. Soon I will be moved to another room, when I am fully dead," she tells me as as she stares at the bed opposite. I want to be able to look at her as she speaks, but I also want to be able to focus on what it is that she is staring at.

I sit alongside and lower my head to the same level as her own as I try to get a better image of what she is seeing. She is looking at three red lights over the bed opposite hers. These are the indicators for the medical equipment for that bed, but Peggy is convinced that these are indicators for her final hours. She tells me that when the last light goes out, she will be dead. I reach out to take her hand and she starts talking again. "It's no use taking my hand. I am dying. When the last light goes out I am dead, I'm telling you. There are lots of comings and goings in this room. It's only a waiting area for those of us who are dying. I almost died yesterday, you know. I went down the long tunnel and I heard my name being called and I saw my brother. I'm only here for a short time more so don't waste your time with me. They won't tell me what is really wrong with me and they are pretending that it is only a broken hip. It's just like what went on with my sister when she had the bone cancer. We didn't know that she was dying. They haven't the guts to tell me the truth."

As she talks, I am anxious that she is talking herself into an early grave. I am digging deep inside myself looking for something intelligent and reassuring to say. It's not at all easy. My heart is beating like a mad drum. All sorts of thoughts are flying around inside me. I want the clock to go back and for none of this to have happened. But here I am sitting beside Peggy and the clock continues to go forward. I can't believe that I'm only worried about the fact that I can't find an intelligent and insightful word to say. I have to pinch myself to stop thinking about my awkwardness in the situation. I stop and listen more closely to Peggy.

At last I remember that Clare told me about how she had visited on the previous day and had seen Peggy on the hospital trolley being wheeled from the surgical ward to this ward. Clare remembered that Peggy was very groggy at the time and didn't really recognise her. I reposition myself and sit directly in front of Peggy, blocking her view of the three red lights. Making eye contact with her, I venture to speak. "Clare was in yesterday. Did you see her?" "No," she answers. "Clare met you when you were being moved from the surgical ward to this ward. This is an orthopaedic ward for patients with bone problems." But she insists "No, it's not. It's a ward for dying people. I'm dying and they won't say it".

I can't believe her persistence with her theory. I glance around the room looking for some support from the other patients. But they are all too sick to get involved. I am alone with Peggy on this one. I try again to make sense of the predicament. "Honestly Peggy, this is not a ward for the terminally ill or a ward for cancer patients. You are here because you broke a bone. This is the orthopaedic ward. There is a large sign on the door to say this and all the patients in here have at least one broken bone. Can I place the glasses on your nose so that you can see a bit more clearly?" I put the glasses on her nose and she looks around. She again sees the red lights opposite and once again I explain that these are for medical equipment. Now that she can see a little more, I point out that other beds also have a set of red lights. She is beginning to accept what I am saying. Then she notices that there is a set of lights over her bed and that there are tubes, bottles and other medical devices connected to these. Her eyes change and seem to regain some of the life I am more accustomed to seeing in them. She asks me to tell her more about what has happened.

"When Clare saw you yesterday, you were groggy and mumbling. That was probably the influence of the anaesthetic. When I had surgery a few years ago, I was totally confused after the anaesthetic. It sometimes takes a few days before you think and reason clearly. It affects us all in different ways. From what Clare saw, you were like a drug addict spaced out on a drug-induced trip!"

Peggy smiles at the notion of being on a drug-induced trip. The smile becomes a laugh which we both share. She has no recollection of the journey on the hospital trolley. She does not remember seeing Clare, but she clearly remembers going down a long dark tunnel. She remembers hearing a voice call her name and she is slowly, very slowly, beginning to accept that the voice that called her name could have been Clare's. At last, she is shifting her attention to me and drifting away from the red lights. "Okay," she says, "maybe it was Clare who called to me, but where is that tunnel?" Smiling, I answer: "There is a long corridor between the new hospital and this section. You were originally admitted to a ward in the new hospital, but now you are in the orthopaedic ward in the old hospital. Did you know you were being moved? Did anyone mention that you would be taken from surgery to a different place?"

She concentrates, trying to remember what was said. She was so tired and in so much pain before the surgery, she cannot really remember anything. She does remember being in a brighter ward. She remembers the staff were different and that there was lots of colour. This new ward is completely different. It is dark and dreary and there are no flowers or cards anywhere. It's like a dungeon compared to what she is used to. Peggy finds it hard to believe that the two wards could be in the same hospital.

It is dawning on her that there is some logic in what I am offering her, but she is reluctant to grasp too tightly at the possibility of a second chance at life. She has convinced herself of her imminent death and she is understandably afraid to look back and choose life. She is so convinced that she is at death's door, I realise it is going to take more effort from the two of us to turn her round completely. So we continue watching each other, listening to each other, answering each other's questions and simply talking to each other. "Are the lights really to do with the equipment?" "Yes they are," I answer, "everybody has three lights and only a few have their lights on." "And the corridor you're talking about, I think I know it – it's a bit like a tunnel, isn't it? But who were the people? I'm sure one of them was my brother who died a few years ago. He was encouraging me to go with him." "The people," I explain, "were other patients, visitors and hospital porters who were chatting with you as they wheeled the trolley and, of course Clare, who actually called you by name."

Peggy is willing to accept that she really is in a hospital ward and not in the 'dying room'. She is no longer trapped in a state of trepidation. She is still anxious though and I think she is a little afraid that I might be lying to her to make her feel better. But I can't lie to her. I won't lie to her. I actually don't understand the notion of lying to help someone feel better. Maybe they help the one telling the lies feel better, but it surely must be only momentary. In Peggy's case, my determination to stay by her and help her see that she is alive and that she has a life to look forward to is something like the determination one might have holding tight to the wrist of a friend who is slipping down a precipice. I put Peggy's confusion down to the anaesthetic and I suggest as much to her. She looks at me for more reassurance. Slowly and very tentatively we piece together the events since her fall the previous week. We are both on the point of tears as we put the final pieces of the jigsaw together. It takes hours, but it is worth it to see her smile as I leave.

I don't know how I stayed with Peggy today. I was so tired and worn out by the confusion she presented. The concentration needed to keep on top of her version of the events was incredible. I wanted to walk out so many times, but something inside me kept me going. I was so afraid that I would say the wrong thing. But how could I say the wrong thing? That something inside me that kept me going during the visit led me on. The words and reasoning were not mine – they came once I stopped concentrating on myself and focused more fully on Peggy. Just one week after the busy Easter weekend, I am in the middle of another Easter story. The readings these days are telling us about Mary Magdalene going to the empty tomb to attend to her Master. I instead went to the hospital to attend to Peggy. I only now make the connection between the two events. Jesus told Mary not to cling to Him because he had not ascended to His Father. Peggy told me not to take her hand because she was not yet dead – dying, but not dead.[4]

I rest overnight and today I enjoy a day in the fresh air. I need the space to gather myself before returning to see Peggy. I walk into the ward and she is not in her bed. I immediately think the worst. I find a nurse and ask her where Peggy is now. I can hear the upset in my voice because, deep down, I believe she is in the mortuary. In just a few seconds, I convince myself that all the previous evening was in vain and that Peggy was right about her 'dying room'. The nurse smiles and tells me that Peggy is in a different ward, back in the new hospital.

---

4 Personal Journal, 29 April 2000

I run over to the new hospital and find Peggy sitting up in bed, smiling. She looks great. The ward is bright and airy and she has her flowers and cards around her again. This is an entirely different woman today, just twenty-four hours after the near-death experience. It is a wonderful visit. She remembers so much of the conversation of last night and she tells me that she honestly believed she was dying. There is a very new relationship between the two of us now. Despite the fact that we know each other for many years, this evening we are talking to each other at a new depth. We have walked a very fine tightrope together and reached the other side safely. We are in every sense, resurrection people. We don't need a lot of words during this visit, but we have lots of smiles and good eye contact. Before I leave, Peggy thanks me for bringing her out of what she calls her "bad patch".

I got such a fright when Peggy wasn't in the orthopaedic ward. I was sure she had died as she had said she would, and that she was now wagging her finger at me from heaven saying – "I told you I was dying". God is playing games with me again. I guess it wasn't the right time for her to ascend to her Father yesterday and I'm really glad – thanks.[5]

Peggy is doing well in hospital. She is improving steadily everyday and I find it hard to believe it is only two weeks since she had the fall. As she improves, I receive word that my good friend Brian is not expected to live beyond the next twelve months. It's a dreadful blow and makes my visits to Peggy that bit more difficult. All the effort to bring Peggy back from the edge, but there will be no bringing Brian back from his edge. Hours before hearing Brian's sad news, I write the following in my journal:

My life is changing so quickly yet there is nothing I can do to stem the flow. Today, I acknowledge the gifts and powers that are God-given. I

5 Personal Journal, 30 April 2000

have the confidence to see the gifts and own them for myself. I have a gift of being able to be with people – a gift which only became fully visible to me when, last weekend, I stayed with Peggy until she "came back to life". God, You gave me a most unusual gift for dealing with this type of pain and also the gift of being able to be authentic in this dreadful place. Why could I not have a gift of being able to be fully in places of utter joy? Of course, these places of pain have their wonderful moments of joy – I know that. Your gifts are precious, but they are frightening and daunting. I am always surprised at how I deal with the situations but I know I am never alone in this work. I know that You work through me because my staying power, my language and my very being is not my own. It's You holding my hand and helping me every step of the way. It's a gift from a higher place. I get so frightened by what I do after I have come through, yet You give me the strength and desire to keep going. I feel utterly alive while I do this work. I feel fruitful even though there are times of intense pain, there are also times of immense joy. I now see the joy and hold on to the memory of it to help sustain me in the bad times. Holding on to the joy keeps me safe in the knowledge that we do this together.[6]

Trying as I do to understand what is happening, I come across St Paul's first letter to the Corinthians.[7] It helps me to accept the gifts and the challenges they present. Peggy and I now have a new

---

6 Personal Journal, 5 May 2000

7 Now there are varieties of gifts, but the same Spirit; and there are varieties of services, but the same Lord; and there are varieties of activities, but it is the same God who activates all of them in everyone. To each is given the manifestation of the Spirit for the common good. To one is given through the Spirit the utterance of wisdom, and to another the utterance of knowledge according to the same Spirit, to another faith by the same Spirit, to another gifts of healing by the one Spirit, to another the working of miracles, to another prophecy, to another the discernment of spirits, to another various kinds of tongues, to another the interpretation of tongues. All these are activated by one and the same Spirit, who allots to each one individually just as the Spirit chooses. (1 Cor12:4-11)

relationship since that memorable first hospital visit. There is a new level of trust and confidence between us. There is an openness I never thought possible. She is out of the general hospital and in a specialist orthopaedic hospital. She is no longer concerned that she might have cancer. She is concentrating on getting well and getting back on her feet. Her target is to get back to work as soon as possible. Her initial fear has given way to blind determination. It's like watching a bud bursting out and revealing an extraordinary flower, strong and vibrant, ready for the new life.

I visit Peggy in the orthopaedic hospital and she is settled in. She no longer has strain etched on her face and she has even found a hairdresser in the hospital. She looks so much better since she can get properly dressed each day and have her hair styled. Her exercise regime is difficult but she is persevering. She is improving so much that arrangements are being made to have her house made more accessible. She is delighted when I tell her that a bed has been set up in her sitting room downstairs and that rails and special bathroom fittings have been installed.

Peggy is home and getting used to moving around the house again. She thought so often that she would never see her home again, and here she is, back in the middle of her friends and neighbours. Like Lazarus, she is brought back to life.

Watching Peggy, I often think about Lazarus and how he was raised from the dead by Jesus to rejoin his sisters Martha and Mary. Did Peggy experience something similar? Did she see herself being taken by the hand out of the tomb? She was so convinced that she was dying a few weeks ago and now she is back in the heart of her friends. She does try to talk about what happened, but she can't. She tells me again and again that she really was dead and that I encouraged her back. I don't want to hear that. I feel a huge responsibility on my shoulders when she says it. I feel huge conflict inside also. Maybe she wanted to die and now she has to try living again. I didn't ask her what she wanted. But how could I sit back and let her go to join the rest of her family in death? I had to fight as I did to keep her in life – didn't I? I also feel so afraid of the power of my few words that 'brought her back'. But why should I be afraid of my few words? Sure was it not a simple smile from a parishioner one day that moved me to start a brand new life for myself? One simple smile and I never looked back. I should just be grateful for the words and the life.[8]

Peggy misses the contact with people and wants to get back to her old routine as soon as she can. She returns to work on a phased basis. She is slower and less confident in herself but she makes great efforts to pick up where she let off. It is now summer and the weather is improving, making it easier for Peggy to get out and about. She walks with the aid of a stick and, for the first time, has to wear trousers and flat shoes to work, instead of her skirts and high heels. The change in work clothes is a big thing for Peggy, but after a while, I think she enjoys being different. She also enjoys her second chance at life and acknowledges openly to friends and neighbours that she is indeed living her 'second chance'. Clare keeps an especially close eye on her and ensures that she is taking proper care of herself.

I watch Peggy's progress and take a back seat as she makes great efforts to return to full health. I feel like a mother reluctantly letting her child grow up and leave the nest. But Peggy is old enough to be my mother. I am trying to be careful not to crowd her but I also want her to know that I am here if she needs me. She is a very independent lady, but I know she relaxes more when she knows that others are looking out for her. I need to step back enough to allow her to

---

8 Personal Journal, 31 May 2000

continue to grow and get well, but not too far so that we can't reach each other.[9]

Another Easter is upon us and Peggy is unwell again. She has been coping so well for the two years since the surgery, but now her breathing is bad and she is finding it hard to sleep. She is once again frightened that she may have cancer and refuses to seek medical help. Finally, she is admitted to hospital and pneumonia is diagnosed. Her greatest fear, cancer, turns out to be pneumonia. She is very relieved, but at times wonders if it can be true. She doesn't really trust that the doctors are telling her the truth, but she wants to believe what she hears. She is in a very confused state and appears to be clutching at the chance of full health, but feeling threatened by her old, great fear, 'the big C'. Peggy knows that, I, along with the rest of my family are also visiting my aunt Teresa, who is being treated in the same hospital.

The prognosis for Teresa, however, is not as hopeful as Peggy's. She is terminally ill and has been told that she has only a few months to live. Peggy hears our sad news and cannot believe what she is hearing about Teresa, someone she has known all her life. To some extent, Peggy feels it is unfair that a much younger person such as Teresa should succumb to cancer, when Peggy herself has survived so many near-misses. It's hard for both patients to come to terms with their situations. It is also hard on their visitors.

I called to see Peggy today and she is so happy to know for sure that she does not have cancer. She is upset to hear that the news is not so good for Teresa. I called to see Teresa as well and she is so accepting of her diagnosis. She does not seem to be afraid – she is a woman of great faith and she is drawing on this faith a lot these days. Teresa asked me what I think the final judgement will be like.

9 Personal Journal, 28 June 2000

All I could think of was marathon day in the city and coming across the finish line hours behind the winner, but still knowing that I was a winner too. This is what I imagine the final judgement to be like and I told her so. She smiled. She remembers my physical pain whenever I complete a marathon race – she has often seen me the day after hardly able to move. Now she has the pain and we both know that she will be a winner real soon. It will come too soon for me – I don't want to think about her crossing the 'finish' line she is headed for. My emotions are all confused – yet again.[10]

I am involved with a local football club and each year we take a group of youngsters away on an exchange programme to America. The children come from the inner city and our hope with these trips is to show them an alternative to anti-social behaviour. I reluctantly take this break away from the hospital visiting, even though a huge part of me would like to stay put. Teresa has been a very large figure in my life. She and I are very alike and she often teases me, saying, "It's in the 501s – in the genes!" Her prognosis is not that great, but I fully believe she will be waiting to hear all the news when I get back home. There is no hesitancy in her to indicate otherwise. I visit Teresa just before I leave and we speak on the phone the night before I depart. She sounds in great form and I am sure that she will be fine for the ten days of the trip.

While I am away I am woken one night with a severe leg cramp. I step out of the bed and the next thing I am aware of is the noise of my head hitting the floor. It sounds like a water melon crashing on a concrete floor. The noise wakes me to full consciousness. I try to look around but can only lie still in the one position. My head hurts so much. For almost an hour I put all my effort into trying to remain conscious. I recite my name over and over again. I recall

---

10 Personal Journal, 20 April 2002

where I am and why I am here. Eventually, I crawl to the kitchen and pull myself up so that I can reach the freezer door. I was advised not to open the freezer by my host because it contains fish bait, but needs must. I pull the solid, frozen bags of fish bait out and apply them to my head.

I remain upright leaning against the wall with the ice pack on my head until morning when my host calls to my room. After the initial shock of finding me in this state, I manage to get ready and join the family for breakfast. I am worried though about the sizeable lump on the back of my head. Since I am travelling with a young group, it is imperative that I join them for the organised events. I agree, however, to return to a party for my host's daughter, Alice, who is graduating from high school. Headaches reminiscent of years before reoccur, but thankfully it is arranged for me to see a doctor who confirms that there is no major damage.

Privately, I am more concerned about how the accident happened and why. I grow concerned about the people back home and try a number of times to contact my family by phone. I have a sick feeling deep down that something awful has happened but don't want to think about it too much. I eventually get through to my mother who is surprised by the call. "Have you heard the news? Did someone get in touch?" she asks. "What news?" I ask. "Teresa – we buried her today. It was very fast in the end. She had a turn for the worst just after you left. We weren't going to tell you until you got home. How did you hear?" I feel myself breaking down but hold on as best I can. I tell her I haven't heard but that I had woken in the night in strange circumstances and guessed something was wrong at home.

I cannot believe that Teresa is gone. It is one thing to talk about the final judgement as being like a marathon race, but now she has crossed the 'finish' line. Why did it all happen while I was so far away? Why could I not have been close by? No goodbyes for us only "See you when I get back". Well I'm back and she's gone. It is like being robbed blind. How do I face the family? How do I face myself? I feel I've let her down, and I also feel she has let me down by not waiting. So it's quits for us – both let down. No goodbyes – but lots of memories. It'll have to be "See you" in my dreams and memories from now.[11]

The reality of returning home to such a changed place is hard to take. But I have to take it on board and I do. I catch up on all the news, good and bad. It's difficult meeting relatives for the first time since missing the funeral. Teresa's sister is somewhat intrigued by the curious incident in the night in America. She suggests that Teresa and I were so close that it is not really surprising. Applying her logic, I often wonder what Teresa did to her enemies if throwing someone across a room is reserved for close friends. It brings a whole new meaning to the expression 'wake up call'.

Peggy is recovering slowly in hospital and is soon to be discharged. She knows about Teresa's death and seems determined to fight and beat her illness. It is a comfort to see her making the effort and I am delighted to hear that she has decided to go to a nursing home to convalesce. She goes directly to the nursing home from the hospital and she is treated really well. She has a lovely room in beautiful surroundings – it is so refreshing and health-inducing. She gets lots of rest and pampering and returns to her home within two weeks, a brand new person.

Peggy is anxious to return to a normal routine as soon as possible. Her health, however, starts to ebb away soon after she returns home from the nursing home. While she is at the nursing home,

11 Personal Journal, 30 May 2002

the nurses ensure that she gets the correct medication at the correct time. When she returns home, it is hard to know if she is able to manage the medication by herself. Even though all the medication is organised for her, I suspect she cannot monitor it properly.

As the days go by, I notice the changes in her. She is breathless again, but this time she is sleeping a lot more and she is retaining fluid. She is not looking after her appearance and seems to have lost interest in so many of the things she once held important. She does not bother eating unless the food is brought in to her. She tells me that she often wakes in the early hours of the morning still in the armchair in her sitting room and has no idea how long she has been sleeping there.

I find the deterioration in Peggy's health very sad. She has lost interest in everything and she is afraid a lot of the time. At the moment, the neighbours and friends are keeping her going, but all of us are growing anxious about her deterioration. I would love her to decide to return to the nursing home, but when I suggest it, she talks about the cost. Her health insurance won't cover her unless she is referred to the nursing home from a hospital. In the meantime, we continue to bring her food and help out as much we can, but we are not medics. None of us want to find her collapsed in the house alone – or worse.[12]

It's late July and Peggy is much worse. The doctor has visited a few times and she now has an oxygen machine in the home to help her breathe. She is sleeping most of the time and looks worse than ever. I talk to her about getting the doctor to call again but the doctor is away for the holiday weekend. It is the last holiday weekend of the summer and hard to find help anywhere. Many of the neighbours who had been calling in are taking their

12 Personal Journal, 29 July 2002

annual holidays. As the team of local helpers begins to disappear, I once again broach the subject of the nursing home. After some negotiating, bordering on nagging, Peggy agrees to check out the availability of a bed in the nursing home and allows me phone on her behalf from her own phone. The woman who answers the phone remembers Peggy from her recent stay and says she can return on the following day. I am so concerned I strongly suggest that Peggy return immediately. The woman registers the concern in my voice and agrees. I leave to allow Peggy time to get packed and ready for the off. I suggest calling back in one hour, but it takes three hours for her to get her stuff together. Each time she does anything, she has to take a rest. Even the effort of putting her shoes on requires another rest. What starts out as a simple process turns into a long haul.

The first weekend in August and most of the people I know are coming and going on holidays. Next weekend I'm off to my brother's wedding and I'll feel happier going, knowing that Peggy is in safe hands in the nursing home. She looked so bad today, I know it is a toss up between Accident & Emergency and the nursing home. Thankfully, the nursing home had a room available – I really did not relish spending a bank holiday in the hospital waiting room, knowing that, most likely, she would not be admitted. The look on the nurse's face as I wheeled Peggy in the foyer of the home, affirmed me in my decision to bring her back. Within minutes, the nurse wheeled Peggy back to her room and started looking after her. I returned home very relieved but anxious about how bad she is and hoping against hope that she is in the right place now. It is so hard to know what to do. It's time once more to trust my gut and let go of "what if I had tried this, or that?"[13]

---

13 Personal Journal, 2 August 2002

I phone the nursing home and hear Peggy had an "okay" night. She is still quite sick though and I am grateful for the support of the staff in the home. Two days later, she is not improving as quickly as the staff or I had hoped. Over the weekend, they are so worried they bring in a doctor to see Peggy. I ask the staff nurse if we should consider taking her to the general hospital and am pleased to hear that the option is being considered. Before going the hospital route though, we agree that Peggy's own doctor should be consulted and she calls out the following day.

Within a week, Peggy is improving. She is sleeping more soundly and her fluid retention is not as pronounced. It is great to see the improvement and it is lovely to be able to have a sensible, unbroken conversation with her again. My relief is short-lived though. I receive a message on the Monday morning to say that Peggy has had a bad turn and that she is in hospital on a life-support machine.

I cannot believe the news today. Peggy was doing so well and now she is on a life-support machine. How quickly things change. I remember the fear on Peggy's face when she was in hospital two years ago and I know how she detested the tubes and wiring at the time. She used to say the cruellest thing ever was having a tube inserted down her throat. And I remember she told the doctor at the time how angry she was and she actually made him promise not to do it again. Now two years later, it's a different doctor in a different hospital and he has no idea about the promise she extracted.[14]

As I drive to the hospital with Clare, I feel anxiety build up inside me. I don't know if I will be able for ICU with all the machinery and the noise. I don't know how I will be able to handle the stress of being in this place where life and death are so precariously balanced. The last time I was in ICU was when my own father

---

14 Personal Journal, 12 August 2002

died and with all my heart I want to be at home feeling safe and protected from all this. Clare and I arrive at ICU and request permission to visit Peggy. Permission is denied because Peggy is being "worked on".

When the nurse comes out to talk to us she tells us that Peggy has had another heart attack and she is not ready for visitors. I am shocked to hear the word "another". I didn't know about any other heart attack. I suggest we leave and return the following day, but she bluntly tells us that this might be the last time we see Peggy alive. The butterflies in my stomach issue their battle cry once more.

Clare and I sit in the waiting room and wait. Neither of us have anything to say. What can we say? The smell, the colours, the atmosphere and everything about the hospital waiting room is imprinted in my memory. There is another group waiting for news, eating snacks from the vending machines while they fight back tears. Indeed this all feels like *déjà vu* and then I realise that is the same hospital in which Natalie died, and even though I saw it in a dream, it all feels very real tonight. The colour of the walls and the intensity of the place is just like I remember it from the dream. I have a sense of closure for my journey with Natalie, being in the same place in which she died for the first time since her death.

When the nurse comes out to us, we look anxiously at her expecting her to tell us the worst. Instead, she brings us to the ICU and tells us where Peggy is. Neither Clare nor I recognise Peggy. She looks dreadful. All the time I have known Peggy, she has been a very slim woman with a graceful walk. Tonight, she looks like a Sumo wrestler connected by tubes to all types of monitors and devices.

I know I shed at least one tear as I stood beside Peggy's bed. I wanted to rip all the tubes out of her and allow her go in peace. I know deep down that she did not want this. Not after all that happened two years ago. But, I also know that every effort must be made to preserve her life. But is this life? She breathes only because of the machine. Her heart relies on another machine. Her feeding is through something else. I haven't a clue about the data on the displays, but it keeps coming and while it does, I know there is still some life there. Clare and I leave, absolutely gutted and in a state of shock. When I get home, I phone a friend of mine and tell him the bad news. He reassures me as best he can, but also reminds me that I have a tough week ahead – a week when Peggy may die and I may need to attend a funeral but may not be able to, and also a week when my brother is getting married, a celebration I must attend. He's right. These are the facts and it's a bitter pill to swallow. I have to put things in perspective, and there is no one like my friend for putting facts out there for me in a very supportive and very caring way. He promises to pray that it will work out – whatever that means.[15]

The neighbours find the change for the worst in Peggy hard to believe. We exchange phone calls and keep each other up to date on her progress. Surprisingly, she remains stable and comfortable for a few days without regaining consciousness. All the machines working on her behalf are paying off.

Clare and I are travelling with the rest of our family to my brother's wedding, but before leaving town, the two of us visit Peggy once more in the hope of seeing an improvement. We arrive at ICU and walk down to the bed. Peggy's eyes are open and tears are rolling down her face. Soon tears are rolling down our faces. She recognises us but cannot talk because of the tubes supporting her breathing. She can only communicate with the movement of her eyelids.

15 Personal Journal, 13 August 2002

We start to bring her up to date on the news. Clare tells her that we are off to the wedding on the following day and suddenly all the machines start to alarm. She calms down when we reassure her that we won't be away for long. We lighten the subject by telling her about the fancy outfits we have for the big day. We don't stay long at all, but as we leave we both feel a lot better as we tell her that we will be back with loads of photographs. I feel ready for the celebration and am happier about setting off.

I have mixed emotions as I leave the hospital. I am delighted with Peggy's progress and pleased to be able to leave town for the wedding knowing she is doing better. There is anxiety too. She is a much weaker and a much-changed woman. I don't think she will be able to care for herself anymore, and I don't believe she will allow others to take care of her. It is yet another choice-less choice – in fact there is no choice at all. As I leave the hospital, I have to hand over all my worries and cares, and accept that this is Peggy's life. As much as I would like to be able to fix her, I can't. I have to resign myself to the fact that I have to trust the system and trust everyone in the system, and trust God most of all. So many people are praying for Peggy – I feel safer now and less alone.[16]

When Clare and I return to our respective homes, we phone around the neighbours and friends telling them the good news. Since Peggy has been unconscious for four days, the hospital suggests we organise visitors for Peggy to help stimulate her so that she may come off the machines with a view to moving her to a regular ward. Without any planning or fancy visitors' rosters, the neighbours pick up on the news and keep vigil with Peggy during the weekend. She improves steadily over the three days and when we get back from the wedding, she is a different person. The nurses and doctors in

16 Personal Journal, 13 August 2002

ICU are very pleased with her progress and are very hopeful that she will be able to move soon to a different ward.

It is good news all round. The wedding was excellent and Peggy is doing much better than expected. It is like a dream – I am almost afraid to believe it can be true. But true it is. When I got home, I phoned my pal who promised to pray for Peggy and for all of us. I told him that his prayers were answered and that Peggy did not die while we were away. Not only did she not die, she is getting better. He was so pleased, but we did not forget all that has happened and the likelihood that she will have another attack.[17]

When I next visit Peggy, all the tubes are gone and she is sitting up in the bed. She is able to talk a little, but her voice is raw, so I don't allow her say too much. I fill her in on all the news of the wedding and it's lovely to see her smile again. Her eyes are bright and she is beginning to look more like her old self. She indicates that she has lots to tell me when she gets her voice back, so I have to wait for her news until my next visit.

Wow, what a difference a week makes. It is going from good to better and best. Just as I shed a tear that first night in ICU, I wanted to shed a few when I saw her sitting up in bed. I went through all the questions around the resuscitation and then I saw her smile. It was worth it. All the effort is worth it just to see her smile and see her bright eyes. I also know that she has given a "do not resuscitate" instruction so that if she has another attack, the staff will not intervene. That's a frightening prospect given all that has happened in the week, but it is her choice at this stage of her life. It still feels to me like playing God, but I also remember very vividly how upset she was during all the time she spent hooked up to the machines. I am reminded of the time with Tom when I could see no reason for all the hanging on

17 Personal Journal, 19 August 2002

when we knew there was only one way out. Well, maybe the smile was what this was all about. I have to leave God to do His work in His time and not mine. There is a strange sense that Peggy really wants to be allowed to go – but peacefully, without the machines connected to her. Now I think she will have her wish – go in peace.[18]

Forty-eight hours after that remarkable afternoon when Peggy was sitting up smiling, the hospital contacts me to let me know that she has passed away peacefully. I do not react at all at first. I simply turn cold and continue with the work I am doing. I try to sort out my thoughts but I can't. I feel sad for myself, but part of me is glad for Peggy that she is not going to lose her independence. As I walk home, neighbours sympathise with me at the loss of Peggy. Reality is beginning to dawn and I don't like that reality. Tears gently stream down my face and there is nothing I can do about them.

For over two years, I have watched Peggy in good times and bad, and now it is over. I remember the night I spent with Peggy two years ago and how the relationship deepened that evening. I remember so many different times and events. Tonight, a few of us gathered to talk about the funeral and the liturgy and all of us agree that she should be given a good send-off. When I got home I spent a lot of time preparing the liturgy. I found readings and wrote prayers that I believed would show the Peggy most people knew. It is really hard, but very helpful for me to take the time to do this. It helps me reflect on the person, honour the person and also acknowledge for myself that we had difficult times and times when we were less than fond of each other. Just sitting in the quiet and reading such supportive and reassuring texts helps me so much. The life is not over with the death. Life is changed and moves to an even deeper level.[19]

---

18 Personal Journal, 21 August 2002
19 Personal Journal, 24 August 2002

The funeral is a very moving ceremony. The neighbours come in force and celebrate Peggy's life. I feel strong until I hear the prayers I have written being read out. Somehow, at this point, the reality is hitting me in a much stronger way. My head knows the facts but now my heart is feeling them too. I can no longer hold back the tears and cry quietly. Before the commendation I read the Cardinal Newman's reflection for the congregation. I want them all to know how we are all linked even though we don't always know it, and that all of these links make us who we are today. As the coffin is carried out by Clare's sons and some of Peggy's cousins, we know that we are lucky to have journeyed with her.

I don't think I ever really knew Peggy. I took each day as it came and trusted that we would come through OK. That attitude worked well two years ago, but this final journey – I'm not sure. Since her passing, I have learned so much about her. I never realised how fond of all of us she was. She rarely showed her feelings, but even now it is lovely for me to know how she felt. It is a shame, though, that she did not know how fond of her so many people were as well, particularly our family. Even still, people talk of her with fondness and miss her.[20]

I chose the Book of Revelation for the funeral Mass because I believe it is true for all of us for when our time comes to 'go in peace'.

Write down: happy are those who die in the Lord! Happy indeed, the Spirit says; Now they can rest for ever after their work, since their good deeds go with them.[21]

---

20 Personal Journal, 24 August 2002
21 Revelation 14:13

SEE YOU

We will remember them[1]

I am not very good at saying goodbye when the time comes to depart so I normally say "See you" with a broad smile, and then walk away. This is the way it has been for as long as I can remember. It is a conscious decision on my part not to use the word goodbye because I firmly believe that I will see the person I am leaving some time in the future. When I meet a person, I am never sure where our journey together will take us, but I do know and believe that every encounter is filled with lessons and opportunities for the personal and spiritual growth of both of us.

Each journey you joined me on in this book ended in death. The deaths brought huge sadness and loss to me, but the lives prior to the deaths were filled with more than a fair share of happiness and fun. Looking back and remembering in faith brings change and growth in my own spiritual and personal journey. I go through times when I believe a passing is 'goodbye', because I know I will never have those special moments with my friends again. We will never share a smile, take a walk together or partake of a cup of tea. But each passing is, in fact, 'see you' because every time I

---

1 Laurence Binyon (1869-1943). They shall not grow old / As we that are left grow old / Age shall not weary them / Nor the years condemn / At the going down of the sun / And in the morning / We will remember them.

remember, I see the person clearly in my memory. It takes time and considerable reflection to accept all that I have lost through their passing before I begin to see the benefits of the times we have shared and all that I have received.

I never plan to journey with a particular person, nor do I plan an outcome or lesson from a journey. I allow all to unfold in its own time, knowing that it will be fine in the end. Today, I continue to journey with the people I meet in the nursing home and in the homeless centre. I also enjoy the journeys with those I meet as I go through my normal daily routine, whether it is in my place of employment or as part of my involvement within my parish. These are the neighbours, friends and complete strangers I meet in my locality and further afield. The lessons learned in the day-to-day encounters are as important to me as the lessons learned in the other journeys.

As I say "See you" at this point, I invite you too, to take the risk to see beyond the simple encounters that you have with each person you meet on your journey every day. I also invite you to be open to the unlimited opportunities that lie beneath the surface of each of these meetings. I wonder how often we look on each meeting as an important part of our personal journey and give ourselves the time to see it all unfold before us.

From my own experiences, I know that one of the wonderful things about making a journey with another human being is that that person is always going to be a part of me. Even though they may not be physically present, I see them in my dreams, in my thoughts and in those private, solitary moments of quiet. Some of the memories are sad and painful while many others are happy and filled with fun. Whatever the memory and whatever the event, they are part of me and make me who I am today. We are all part of the universe, members of the human race and humanity, and the smallest molecule is an intrinsic part of us, even though we may never know that molecule. St Paul puts it like this:

For just as the body is one and has many members, and all the members of the body, though many, are one body, so it is with Christ. For in the one Spirit we were all baptised into one body – Jews or Greeks, slaves or free – and we were all made to drink of one Spirit. Indeed, the body does not consist of one member but of many. If the foot would say, "Because I am not a hand, I do not belong to the body," that would not make it any less a part of the body.[2]

Thank you for giving me the opportunity to share these love stories with you. As you can see, love comes with its fair share of sorrow. In each and every one of these relationships, the love experienced outlives the sorrow. My hope is that you too will experience the love long after the sorrow dissipates. And remember, it is not "Goodbye", rather it is "See you" for those we meet will always be part of us long after the departures.

I am many ways of being in one person
Just as the sun, moon and stars form parts of the sky
So my many ways of being form parts of my life.
They are visible in varying ways.
Just as night unfolds to reveal a new day
So God's plan for my life unfolds through my connections with others
And others unfold through my connections with them.
I did not know them yesterday
We only found each other today
We have no history – only now
We have eternity together because of now.[3]

---

2 1 Corinthians 12:12-14
3 Personal Journey, 20 February 2004